Practical
Guide
to
Christian
Living

Practical Guide to Christian Living

Michael Scrogin

Judson Press ® Valley Forge

Acknowledgments and Credits

"The Pauper Witch of Grafton" from "Two Witches" in *The Poetry of Robert Frost*, edited by Edward Connery Lathem. Copyright 1923, © 1969 by Holt, Rinehart & Winston. Copyright 1951 by Robert Frost. Reprinted by permission of Holt, Rinehart and Winston, Publishers.

The Awful Rowing Toward God, by Anne Sexton. Copyright © 1975 by Loring Conant, Jr., Executor of the Estate of Anne Sexton. Reprinted by permission of Houghton Mifflin Company.

Twentieth Century Journey, by William L. Shirer. Copyright 1976 by William L. Shirer. Reprinted by permission of Don Congdon Associates, Inc.

Excerpt from "The Dummy" from *I, Etcetera*, by Susan Sontag. Copyright © 1963, 1978 by Susan Sontag. Reprinted by permission of Farrar, Straus and Giroux, Inc.

Breathing Tokens, by Carl Sandburg. Copyright © 1978 by Maurice C. Greenbaum and Frank M. Parker, Trustees of the Sandburg Family Trust. Reprinted by permission of Harcourt Brace Jovanovich, Inc.

"Leaving the Yellow House" in *Mosby's Memoirs and Other Stories* by Saul Bellow. Copyright © 1967 by Saul Bellow. Reprinted by permission of Viking Penguin Inc.

Mr. Sammler's Planet by Saul Bellow. Copyright © 1969, 1970 by Saul Bellow. Reprinted by permission of Viking Penguin Inc.

Unless otherwise indicated, Bible quotations in this volume are from the Revised Standard Version of the Bible copyrighted 1946, 1952 © 1971, 1973 by the Division of Christian Education of the National Council of the Churches of Christ in the U.S.A., and used by permission.

Other Bible quotations are from the *Good News Bible*, the Bible in Today's English Version. Copyright © American Bible Society, 1976. Used by permission.

Library of Congress Cataloging in Publication Data

Scrogin, Michael.
    Practical guide to Christian living.

    Bibliography: p.
    1. Christian life—Baptist authors. 2. Decision-
making (Ethics) I. Title.
BV4501.2.S348 1985   248.4'861   84-27773
ISBN 0-8170-1053-X

For my parents,
Bill and Jane Scrogin,
who were always there when I needed them,
and who taught me love by living it.

Contents

Introduction

Times of important decision making are often agonizing. We know the choice before us is terribly important. But that is almost all we know. Standing at the fork in the road, we can't see far enough down the paths that branch off to know with certainty where any one leads. We easily find ourselves confused, numbed, and depressed at such crucial times of choices. Just when faith, energy, and courage are most needed, they seem least present in our lives.

This book is addressed to anyone who is faced with an important decision. It is written out of the conviction that the Christian faith, and specifically the Gospels, is a rich and dependable guide and resource at any time of major choice in life. In the course of the book I explore from a Christian point of view the elements that go into a good decision, the resources our faith provides at such a time of choosing, and the dangers and pitfalls that threaten at these decision points.

The idea for the book and the specific issues explored in it have grown up out of my work as a pastor and counselor. Or to put it more directly, most of the ideas and insights the book contains are not my own. They were given to me by friends in the congregations I've served. It is a great privilege to be a pastor. I am especially grateful to all those persons who have shared their lives and their decisions with me in the community of faith. They have been the best, most loving teachers I have ever had. I won't name names—that would be too personal—but I will name churches. My thanks go to the members of the First Baptist Church of Newton, Massachusetts, who endured me as a raw, new associate pastor; to the beloved people of University Baptist and Brethren Church, State College, Pennsylvania, who listened while I learned to preach; and to my friends, the members of the First Baptist Church of Worcester, Massachusetts, who continually give me all the loving support a pastor could need.

Michael Scrogin
Worcester, Massachusetts
1984

SECTION 1

What Goes into Making a Decision

1

How to Make the Best Decision

Now great multitudes accompanied him; and he turned and said to them, "If any one comes to me and does not hate his own father and mother and wife and children and brothers and sisters, yes, and even his own life, he cannot be my disciple. Whoever does not bear his own cross and come after me, cannot be my disciple. For which of you, desiring to build a tower, does not first sit down and count the cost, whether he has enough to complete it? Otherwise, when he has laid a foundation, and is not able to finish, all who see it begin to mock him, saying, 'This man began to build, and was not able to finish.' Or what king, going to encounter another king in war, will not sit down first and take counsel whether he is able with ten thousand to meet him who comes against him with twenty thousand? And if not, while the other is yet a great way off, he sends an embassy and asks terms of peace. So therefore, whoever of you does not renounce all that he has cannot be my disciple" (Luke 14:25-33).

Is there an important decision facing you? I mean a major, life-changing decision, not just a minor choice—a decision about home or career, school or college, marriage or family, business or finances, retirement, a move, life or death?

If so, how are you going to reach that decision? How will you find strength to face it, wisdom to examine it fully, and faith to see you through your choice? Quite often it's not so much that we do something about reaching decisions as that they do something with us, like ruin our sleep, give us ulcers, or drive us to drink. Quite often, in fact, we silently suffer as the decision that waits to be made simply looms there in its menacing, no-nonsense, not-about-to-go-away manner. We tell no one what's worrying us, not even close friends or family. We may be so consumed by worry that we don't even calm ourselves long

13

enough to reach out in prayer for hope and guidance. Huge, demanding decisions come steamrolling into our lives and, because we've only lived this life one time, we are quite naturally surprised by them. What do we do?

Our belief as Christians is that decisions do not come into our lives by accident. We believe even the unpleasant decisions are put in our path, often quite immovably, by God. Does that mean that God wants to make us suffer, to hurt us? No. Does it mean that God is merely testing us, toying with us, seeing if we can complete the task before us? No. It means that God wants to reinforce a promise given to us, a promise that can stand through every time of decision—namely, that no matter what, God will go with us through that hard season. Often we'd like a different kind of promise, wouldn't we? We'd like it very much if God would remove the decision from us, decide it for us and tell us what to do. But that is emphatically *not* what God has promised. The promise that is explicit in Jesus Christ is that God is with us; even through the difficult times—and especially there—the Spirit will be present with us and will not force us to make those decisions by ourselves. Is there a decision facing you?

The First Danger: Avoidance

The first impulse, perhaps, when a major choice comes up in life is to avoid it—to try to deny it. The first temptation is to pretend that the decision is not part of our life and that we don't have to do anything. Saul Bellow has a marvelous short story entitled "Leaving the Yellow House." It's the tale of Hattie Simmons Waggoner, an elderly woman who lived alone in a house that she inherited. It was all she had and was everything to her. The woman who willed it to Hattie was now dead. All Hattie's family was gone. She had no children or husband. Living alone and becoming increasingly frail, she turned in on herself, and turned also to drinking too much. She, of course, knew that she had to make a change. She could not continue in that big rambling house. She had to go somewhere else, to leave the house (that's one of the meanings of the title "Leaving the Yellow House"), and she had to leave it *to* someone in her will. That's the other meaning of the story's title. She knew this, but for years did nothing about it.

Then, one day, driving while drunk, she had a minor traffic accident. Her arm was broken. Her license was taken away. She recovered, but the arm was slow to heal. Friends came to tell her that she had to leave, had to get out—still she couldn't. One night, thinking that she'd finally come to a decision, she sat down and began to write a will:

"I, Harriet Simmons Waggoner, being of sound mind and not knowing what may be in store for me at the age of seventy-two (born 1885), living alone at Sego Desert Lake, instruct my lawyer, Harold Claiborne, Paiute County Court Building, to draw my last will and testament upon the following terms."[1]

She lifted a pencil from the page, thought a bit, took a drink, realized that she spent all her life waiting. She thought to herself,

I was waiting, thinking, "Youth is terrible, frightening. I will wait it out. And men? Men are cruel and strong. They want things I haven't got to give."[2]

Then she turned again to write the will:

"Upon the following terms . . . Because I have suffered much. Because I only lately received what I have to give away. . . . It is too soon! Too soon! . . . Even though by my own fault I have put myself into this position. And I am not ready to give up on this. No, not yet. And so I'll tell you what, I leave this property, land, house, garden, water rights, to Hattie Simmons Waggoner. Me! I realize this is bad and wrong. Not possible. Yet it is the only thing I really wish to do, so may God have mercy on my soul."[3]

In her hour of extremity and need, all she could think to do was to try insanely to leave the house to herself, to perpetuate a tragic situation. She could not accept and would not choose the decision that was forcing itself upon her. She could not leave the house.

Perhaps, like Hattie Waggoner, we have avoided the decision in front of us for too long. Perhaps we have reached the point now where the decision can be avoided further only at our peril and at the expense of hurting others. That's the first temptation we face when decisions enter our lives—we will try to wait them out; we will wait too long.

A Second Danger: Coercion

A second error we easily make when a decision comes into our lives is to hurry it, to rush it. It's very tempting to try to force a decision, to bring our worry and uncertainty to an end, or to find someone who will force the decision on us. Make no mistake. There are plenty of people around who are glad to give ironclad advice about what we should do, often in the name of religion. On October 21, 1982, this small article appeared in *The New York Times* in the section called "Washington Talk":

> Raymond A. Peck, head of the National Highway Traffic Safety Administration, returned to Washington yesterday from Chicago looking like a man who had picked a fight with a motorcycle gang and lost. [Mr. Peck] was addressing the National Safety Council in Chicago when a man in the audience stood up and began railing against President Reagan and his policies. The highway safety chief tried to humor the man, let him ramble a bit. Then suddenly the heckler hurled a book right at Mr. Peck, knocking off his glasses and cutting his brow. The book that inflicted the nine-stitch wound was a Bible.[4]

Sometimes we are tempted to force a decision or to let someone else force a decision on us. At our worst and weakest we can look to our religion as an inflexible, iron code with an answer to every question, rather than seeing Christianity for what it truly is—a living, breathing, and subtly guiding presence in our lives. At our worst we want to throw the Bible at others or hit ourselves stupidly over the head with it, as if faith were a weapon rather than a promise, a coercive lever that could force us in God's direction, rather than a still, small voice calling to us in the dark.

Does a decision face you? One temptation is to let it drag on too long and not to make it in time. The other is to try to force it or let someone force it so that it doesn't grow up naturally in you. Neither of these ways is from God. Neither leads toward God.

The Best Decision

How can you make the best decision? Consider the passage that opened this chapter. It is one of the very hard sayings of Jesus, one that we don't like to hear. In it there are four paradoxes, or four tensions, that need to be present in our lives in any season of decision, in any time of making hard choices.

The First Paradox

The first paradox is this: *The guides and landmarks of the past may not serve well in the future. But, still, you must take your past with you.*

You can't move into a new situation based only on the past. Listen to what the Scripture says. Great crowds were following Jesus. He turned to them, saying, "Whoever comes to me cannot be my disciple unless he hates his father and his mother, his wife and his children, his brothers and his sisters and himself as well." *Hates his father and his mother . . . his brothers and his sisters and himself as well.* Does Jesus really mean hate father and mother? No. (To you teenagers, especially, please know he does not mean that. That's why all of us can get into such trouble interpreting the Bible only literally.) Jesus lived in the Middle East, and in his day as well as in our day (you can see it in any newspaper account) language was often extravagant. People spoke in a way that would get someone's attention, draw listeners up short.

The word that Jesus uses for "hate" really means "to love less." Matthew 10:37 translates it that way: "Unless you love your father or mother less than me you cannot be a disciple." What's implied is that those past ties can't always take you into the future that your decision requires. There is something more than the old, the usual, the customary, the things that your parents taught you. Something more than that will have to take you into the future. That's half of the paradox. The past guides don't always work, nor are they always sufficient. The other half of that paradox is that the past must go with you into the future. You simply can't abandon it. You can't run away from it. You can't ignore it.

Carl Sandburg has a poem entitled "An Old Woman." It's a poem about and for his mother. In it he remembers his departure, as a young man, from home and from her:

> Looking on the open
> Glow of a full-golden moon
> In the drowsy, almost noiseless
> Dream-watch peace of midnight
> In a prairie town, she
> Touched me with her lips and hands
> and babbled softly she would
> Listen till the sound of my footsteps
> Was gone.
>
> I kissed my hand to the dim shape
> Standing in the shadows under the porch
> Looking good-by to her boy
> And I keep a picture

Of one shaft of moonlight
Trembling near her face
Telling of wishes farther than love or death,
The infinite love of an old woman
Keeping a hope for her boy.[5]

Sandburg knew that in his leaving he had to put past behind. He also knew that a great deal of the past went with him. He knew that in any relationship of love with a parent or someone as important as a parent, there are "wishes farther than love or death." Those wishes, those long-held loves, will certainly, must certainly go with you and me into a new future we decide upon. When any great decision confronts us, the paradox is that on the one hand the past cannot be an entirely sufficient guide and on the other, the past must go with us into that future and cannot be completely left behind.

The Second Paradox

A second paradox, or tension, is that *suffering, an inherent element in a hard decision, is also that which is redemptive in the decision.*

Jesus says, "Whoever does not carry his own cross and come after me, cannot be my disciple." The first part of this tension, this paradox, is that there will be a cross and that you must carry it; no one else will, no one else can. Suffering is a part of any hard decision. If it weren't, there wouldn't be any decision to make, would there? If there weren't some suffering, some difficulty there, you would simply go on with your life of ease and there would be no problem, no threshold to cross. The presence of suffering, of pain in our lives, is often a clue, a signal, a sign that decision time is due or overdue.

On the one hand, as Christ tells us, you can expect that cross to be there. On the other, that same cross will heal you. The suffering that you go through will be, must be, redemptive, or else it is not from God. How often do you hear people say about some problem in life, "We all have our cross to bear." It's a cliché. And it's all wrong. Not all suffering that comes to us is a cross. Some of it is wasteful, meaningless pain—pain that we ought to be able to get out of or to avoid. Not all suffering is from God, but some is. How can you tell the difference? *The suffering that has hope on the other side—that is from God.* That's what the cross is about. The cross leads not merely to death but to resurrection, not merely to agony but to new life.

One of the things that often grips many of us who are facing decisions is a kind of paralysis. We look at our lives; we look at the choices available and every possible option is painful. Not a single option avoids a significant amount of hurt. In such a situation it is only natural to duck the head, hold on, and hope to avoid making any choice. Paralysis sets in—paralysis because we haven't yet asked the right question. The right question is not whether the choice hurts or doesn't hurt, but which of those painful choices has a hopeful outcome? Many of us have been through seasons of illness when the only way we could come through and be well again was to go under the surgeon's knife. I do not know anyone who welcomes such a time. We knew it was the right thing to do, didn't we, because it had a hope of healing on the other side of the pain? If the choice that stands in front of you means only a continuation of the pain and nothing more—no renewal and no hope—that pain is not from God. If the pain is there, but on the other side of it is or might be renewal, such pain is what the cross is about.

So the second paradox or tension: suffering is indeed part of any great decision, but not all suffering is from God. Only that suffering with a hopeful possibility on the other side of it is from God.

The Third Paradox

A third paradox, or tension, is that *the best decision will be costly; yet you will have the assets to meet it.*

Jesus said, "If one of you is planning to build a tower, he sits down first and figures out what it will cost in order to see if he has enough money to finish the job." The great decisions force us to count the cost, to ask whether we have enough reserves— spiritual, emotional, personal—to face them. Great decisions are always costly. Of course, we already know that, don't we! We see those come-ons in the magazines, for example, those offers that come to us that aren't supposed to cost anything and we know immediately they are fraudulent. We see advertisements that say, "Give me five minutes a day for six weeks and you can have a totally new body." We don't sign up for those things because they have no cost associated with them and can't possibly be meaningful opportunities. Or maybe you have seen an ad for the book *How to Pick Up Girls,* which has appeared in *The*

New York Times Magazine. The author lists thirty phrases that drive women wild. I'm not sure what they are. One of them that drives women wild in my experience is, "But can she type?" However, I don't think that's what the author is talking about. Again, we know that sort of thing is fraudulent because it asks for nothing from the person who's going to do the picking up. We know it's false. Or we see those offers that show up very regularly on matchbook covers, "Looking for a new career? Try accounting." You open the matchbook and read, "With only two hours a day, in three months time by correspondence, you can become an accountant and earn thirty to forty thousand dollars a year. Close cover before striking." You don't send off for it because there's no cost associated. The great decisions have a cost and we are asked, indeed asked by Jesus himself, to count the cost.

Let us remember that when we count the cost, part of the process means also counting our assets. That part is easily forgotten in any decision. We face something difficult in front of us. We stop to count the cost, but far too quickly we become overwhelmed. We decide we're not equal to it. We start to back down. Implied in Jesus' teaching is not only that we count the cost but also that we count our assets. What has God already put in our hands?

While on vacation and away from my own church, I worshiped at a church where I once had worked. I saw a number of old friends, one of whom was a woman named Jean Nelson. When I'd last seen Jean, she had just gone through a painful divorce. She had moved out of the home she had lived in all her life, moved away from her former husband and her parents and into a small apartment. Back then one could tell every time one saw her that she was lost, tragically so. She didn't know what to do with herself and felt she had nothing to do or be and nowhere to go. She knew only that she had to get out of the marriage; but what the future held, of that she had no idea. It was remarkable to see her after some eight years had passed. She didn't look like the same woman anymore. Though eight years older, she looked much younger. She stood erect and dressed well. Her gray hair was beautifully coiffed. She had become the assistant registrar at one of the major universities in Boston, a job that she never imagined she could have done or even aspired to. I asked her about the job. She said that it had taken some time, but finally she discovered that all those years of organizing the budget and the children and the family, all the years of keeping everything running, had made her a very good administrator, the kind of person that businesses and universities want on their staffs.

It was interesting. During the years of pain and disappointment, of failure and lost love, something was growing in Jean, which she did not recognize or value at the time—the ability to care effectively for others even when not cared for in return, the ability to organize and provide for the physical needs of a large active family. What had been a zero in her accounting process suddenly became a plus and was put over on the credit side. When she counted the cost of what lay before her, she was able to meet the future because she found assets that God had put in her hands, assets that she had forgotten before. So, the third paradox: the best decision will be costly and you must count the cost, but you must not forget to count the assets that God has already given. The chances are that God has put in your hands the resources that you need to make the decision.

The Fourth Paradox

A fourth paradox, or tension, is that *the best decision means saying farewell to some parts of life that have been important as one says hello to what comes afterward.*

Sometimes deciding means saying farewell to much loved people, places or jobs. It also means a "hello," a welcome. Jesus says, "None of you can be my disciples unless he renounces everything he has." It helps to know what the Greek word is for "renounce." The word is *apotassetai* and it can mean "to renounce," but its more frequent meaning is simply "to say farewell," "to wave good-bye." There is a kind of saying farewell that goes with any great decision. It says that the past is past and is no longer present and is no more in control of your life. "None of you can be my disciples unless he says farewell to everything he has." That's part of the paradox but the other part is that saying farewell is not all of it. There is also saying hello—a meeting, an encounter, that comes on the other side of that decision after the farewell has been said.

Let me share a story about myself. From the age of thirteen to twenty, I wanted nothing more than to be a very good football

player. It was my life quite literally. It seems ridiculous now but
it was. I spent hours and hours playing football and many days
and sleepless nights thinking about it. Like everyone else on
the team I aspired to being a professional football player. Things
went well. I did well enough in high school; I was large. I went
to college and played football. Things went well there too—all
the way through my junior year—and then something happened. I don't know what it was exactly, but something changed
between that junior and senior year; something changed within
me. What I had always wanted—one day to have a chance to
play professional football—ceased being important. It simply
dropped out of my life's equation.

I'd been elected captain and I did enjoy the game; so I stayed
with the team during my senior year and played, even played
reasonably well. I can remember a time about three or four games
into the season when Norris Patterson, the coach, called me into
his office and asked what was up. He had watched the game
films, and he knew I wasn't playing like I used to. I had no
intensity. He wasn't saying that he wanted to replace me or that
I wouldn't start, or anything like that, but he was just asking
what had happened. I told him I didn't know what had happened, but football was not as important as it had been. (Please
understand, I'm not advocating this for others. I suppose football
can be a wonderful career. All I'm saying is that it wasn't for
me.) At the end of the season when awards came and when
phone calls came from pro scouts, they didn't interest me a bit.
I entered a period of life that had some considerable confusion.
I didn't know what I was going to do. The dream that had
guided me was cold and dead. I had to say good-bye to it. It
was this saying farewell that led finally to the decision to go to
seminary to become a minister. I didn't see that at the time of
saying good-bye to the dream. All I saw was the pain and
confusion. Now, seventeen years later, I see the joys of saying
hello to God's new choice in my life.

Where is a decision confronting you? The temptation is to try
to avoid it. Or the temptation is to try to coerce it, to hit yourself
or someone else with the Bible, to force a choice. The promise
of God is that that decision is there for your health and that
God will go through that moment, that season, with you.

2

On Asking the Right Question

As he passed by he saw a man blind from his birth. And his disciples asked him, "Rabbi, who sinned, this man or his parents, that he was born blind?" Jesus answered, "It was not that this man sinned, or his parents, but that the works of God might be made manifest in him. We must work the works of him who sent me, while it is day; night comes, when no one can work. As long as I am in the world, I am the light of the world." As he said this, he spat on the ground and made clay of the spittle and anointed the man's eyes with the clay, saying to him, "Go, wash in the pool of Siloam" (which means Sent). So he went and washed and came back seeing. The neighbors and those who had seen him before as a beggar said, "Is not this the man who used to sit and beg?" Some said, "It is he"; others said, "No, but he is like him." He said, "I am the man." They said to him, "Then how were your eyes opened?" He answered, "The man called Jesus made clay and anointed my eyes and said to me, 'Go to Siloam and wash'; so I went and washed and received my sight." They said to him, "Where is he?" He said, "I do not know" (John 9:1-12).

Questions. Questions. Questions. An array of questions always accompany any major decision. We wonder: "Can I avoid or sidestep this choice?" We worry: "When is the right time to act?" We lament: "Why didn't I deal with this sooner?" We kid ourselves: "Do you suppose it will all blow over or go away?" Every time of consequential important decision is surrounded by such a cloud of questions that sometimes the questions themselves, because of their sheer number and stridence, keep us from getting on with what needs doing. The difficulty in such a time is not so much making sure we've considered every question as it is focusing upon the right question. We need to ask that question, the right one, over and over until out of our asking some guidance and hope from God emerges. Scientific advancement, as well as healthy personal choices, has hinged in this century on asking the right question. The great breakthroughs have come not so much because scientists simply gathered more and newer information but because a particular thinker or group of thinkers began looking at the same old data and asking the right questions. This sounds easy, but it is not easy at all because the wrong questions are often quite attractive and look very good and the right ones sometimes are small and well concealed.

Horace Freeland Judson in his remarkable book *The Eighth Day of Creation* recounts the history of molecular biologists' efforts to understand life at its most elemental level. He tells the long, twisting story of how James Watson, Francis Crick, and a handful of other scientists gradually came to understand the structure and activity of DNA in living cells and how they broke the genetic code.

Two Europeans who played major roles in this discovery were Francois Jacob and Jacques Monod. Working together at their Paris laboratory, they took the information that Crick and Watson had supplied about the double-helix structure of DNA and sought to understand specifically how these genetic instructions made new DNA, which has to happen every time a cell divides.

Jacob was convinced that the chemical mechanism involved was what he called an "on-off" switch. Some triggering molecule turned on a switch in the DNA molecule that was to reproduce, causing it to replicate itself. (It turns out that Jacob was right but at the time this theory was far from proven.) Jacob had conducted several experiments to show that a certain triggering chemical would turn on the switch in DNA and the molecule would reproduce itself. He had been partially successful—but his friend, colleague, and competitor Jacques Monod didn't buy Jacob's theory about the switch. In fact, said Monod, Jacob's own experiments showed it couldn't be a simple "on-off" switch. Why? Because, said Monod, the DNA did not reproduce itself at a uniform rate. Its rate of reproduction varied throughout the experiment. Such variance proved, said Monod, that the "on-off" theory wouldn't work. For if the choices were only "on" or "off," the rate should have been constant. It wasn't: ergo, Jacob was on the wrong track.

This troubled Francois Jacob. He put aside his theory for a time, figuring he wasn't asking the right question after all. He started asking instead why the rate of replication fluctuated. This led nowhere.

Then one night at home Jacob stood watching his son playing with an electric train. Here's what he says of that evening:

> The train was a simple set with a switch but no rheostat for regulating the strength of the current to change the speed. My son wanted to slow the train down, and I saw he was doing that— simply by turning the switch back and forth, on and off. Just an oscillation. And depending on the speed of the oscillation he could regulate the rate. And this was my argument which in September I exposed to Jacques. For hours![1]

Jacob had the right question but nearly lost it. He almost let it get away from him, but was saved by a small simple experience of watching his son play at home.

Asking the right question is deeply important on the spiritual side of life as well, for very regularly we organize ourselves around a single, central guiding question that can give meaning and hope to life, such as "What does the Lord require of me?" or "How can I be more faithful?" But it's not always so easy choosing and staying with that right question.

The problem is that there are several very attractive, appealing alternatives that look like they'd have to be the right question to ask. They look like it, but are not—because they do not finally lead to life and growth but to death and cynicism. There are three wrong questions, impostors, pretenders which look good for us but aren't. Many have chosen to live by one of them. These three questions each begin with the phrase "What's wrong with . . . ":

"What's wrong with them?"
"What's wrong with the system?"
"What's wrong with me?"

Are any of these wrong questions deflecting you from the decision toward which God is calling you? Let's examine them.

What's Wrong with Them?

The central question for Judaism and for most people in Jesus' day was "What's wrong with them?" The very system of reli-

gious laws that all Jews, including Jesus, grew up with and
knew was organized around that guiding question. The 613
precepts, i.e., the basic rules of Judaism, were oriented toward
pointing out what was wrong in someone's behavior: What
specific rule had a sad, unacceptable man or woman violated to
displease God? You can see this question behind the disciples'
thinking in John 9:2.

Jesus and the disciples were walking in Jerusalem. They saw
a man who had been blind from birth. Out popped the central
question; in fact the disciples lacked even the sensitivity to realize
how cruel this question must sound. They didn't ask, "How
can we help?" They asked, in essence, "What's wrong with
him?" Their actual words were, "Master, whose sin caused this
man's blindness; his own or his parents'?" There it was. The
big religious enterprise of Jesus' day was assigning blame—
subdividing, labelling, specifying precisely why a certain unfortunate soul was in trouble with God.

Note at the outset that Jesus rejected the whole procedure.
"What's wrong with him?" asked the disciples. "Who sinned,
this man or his parents?" "Neither," answered Jesus, for that
was the wrong question. Rather, one needed to ask how God's
power might be shown in this man. After asking the right
question, Jesus made a poultice of mud, applied it to the blind
man's eyes, and healed him.

This wrong question didn't end with Jesus' day. It is still in
our own generation a mainstay of judgmental religion, much of
which goes under the name of Christianity, unfortunately. On
any Sunday in thousands of churches, you can still hear this
sad, crippling, self-righteous religion preached, the religion not
of God's power in life but of "what's wrong with them?" Why
did their marriage fail, their business turn sour, their son have
trouble with the law, their daughter get pregnant at thirteen?
The whole pitiful litany of misdeeds is recited and the conclusion
drawn that it must have been some flaw, some weakness, or
some sin which had displeased God and brought down judgment. Many churches are organized around the question "What's
wrong with them?"

Many people organize their lives around that same question.
You know some undoubtedly—those sorry, unforgiving souls
who talk of love but never tire of pointing out the flaws, vices,

and misdeeds of others. They talk of forgiveness and are only too glad to offer it after they've made it painfully clear exactly what hideous behavior they are forgiving and have further pointed out that many others, less Christian than themselves, would find it completely impossible to forgive such crimes. They talk of grace and God's redeeming love but make it sound as if these items are so valuable and in such short supply that they are rationed only to the righteous few.

The popular religion today is a faith that upholds as central the ancient question that Jesus chose to oppose in his own day. "What's wrong with them?" And certainly you and I can understand its appeal: In simple terms the one who chooses this guiding, organizing question can put himself or herself up by putting others down. Then, too, it is so easy to find things wrong with other people if that is your interest. Try it yourself. Walk down any street in your neighborhood and glance unobtrusively at every house on the block (don't be too obvious now; one of the neighbors may call the police). In every case, if you make the effort, you'll be able to find something you don't like. The Schwartzes' house needs painting. The Roses' house is the wrong color green. The Abruzzis should do something about those shutters. The Cosgroves's yews are turning brown. The Philbricks should get rid of that ugly birdbath.

There is nothing on earth easier than being a critic. It costs nothing, risks nothing, and finally gives nothing to others or to oneself. "What's wrong with them?" is one of the tempting but unhealthy questions on which we all too easily choose to center our lives. Has it been your question for too long?

What's Wrong with the System?

"What's wrong with the system?" is certainly the question much of the world has chosen as central. Communists find their guidance by asking what's wrong with the capitalist system. Capitalists gain great joy in reciting the wrongs of communism. Revolutionaries of every political bent examine the systems of government, economics, and education under which they live and ask, "What's wrong here?" Then they take up arms to destroy the old and build the new. Regularly the new system simply recreates under new management the sad old patterns of the past.

"What's wrong with the system?" is a popular, convenient

guiding question, but not altogether a bad question. It is worth asking. Systems of government, of economics, of education, of life do have flaws and can use critical examination. My point is not that the question is wrong, but rather that it is not right enough, not good enough to take the place of life's central and guiding concerns.

You can see the question's insufficiency in the lives of many who came of age in the sixties. The theme of that turbulent decade was certainly "What's wrong with the system?" Everyone had a plan to change the world, to take society apart and rebuild from the ground up. While in many ways that time of protest and change was full of energy and hope, much of the energy ultimately was dissipated and many of the hopes proved false. Those who stood at the center of all this turmoil, those who had the highest hopes, also paid the highest price. For in many cases those leaders of the sixties discovered in the late seventies and mid-eighties that this central question, which gave so much energy to their lives for a time, finally left a great spiritual void in their lives. Where have some of these people turned in recent years?

Rennie Davis, an organizer of antiwar protests and a member of the Chicago Seven, has moved from politics to religion and become an official of the Divine Light Mission, a cult which preaches the supremacy of the Maharaj Ji, a young Indian holy man. Abbie Hoffman, another of the Chicago Seven, drifted from political protest into drug use, then lived underground for several years, served a jail term, and has now, upon his release, written a book. Jerry Rubin, organizer of the Youth International Party (the Yippies) and the clowning child of the sixties, has grown very serious in the eighties. He is a Wall Street stockbroker. (It's amazing how much better the system looks now than then.) Eldridge Cleaver, a founder and spokesman for the Black Panther Party, flirted with communism for a while, underwent a dramatic conversion experience, and is now making his living as a fundamentalist Christian evangelist. Bob Dylan, the musician and poet of the sixties' generation, has also converted to fundamentalist Christianity.

Why all this belated spiritual searching among these who once organized their lives around that central question of "What's wrong with the system?" The searching exists today because

the question finally betrayed them. Systems do need changing.
Injustice must be corrected. Peace must be promoted. However,
the changing of systems will not by itself save humankind, nor
will it ever finally meet the deep, inner needs that inhabit the
human soul. It is the wrong question to have at center, though
millions today worship at its altar.

What's Wrong with Me?

The columnist Ann Landers receives twelve million letters
each year—twelve million letters asking advice or simply com-
menting on every conceivable topic, problem, and complaint
that human beings in America can live with. In a recent interview, David Brinkley asked her: "What's the most frequent
question people ask in letters to you?" Miss Landers replied:
"What's wrong with me?" "I'm a teenager and can't get a date
for the basketball game. What's wrong with me?" "I'm sixty-
seven and a widow, but my children never write and seldom
visit; what's wrong with me?" "I'm married to a wonderful man;
we have three beautiful children, a lovely house, and plenty of
money yet I am constantly unhappy. What's wrong with me?"
"I have been married and divorced three times; what's wrong
with me?" "I'm bright and talented and work hard, but I never
get the promotion I want; what's wrong with me?" "I have just
found out that my son uses marijuana; what's wrong with me?"

"What's wrong with me?" More than any other question, this
is the characteristic organizing, guiding question of Americans
in the 1980s. You can hardly be alive and "normal" in this
generation and fail to feel the pull of this question occasionally
on your own life.

If we let it become the central question in our lives, it will
send us on endless, far-from-satisfying errands in search of
something to make us better, to make us whole and right again.
The question will send some people to the shopping mall or car
dealer to buy some temporary relief from the growing anxiety.
"A new outfit might cover what's wrong with me," they say,
"or perhaps in another car I'd feel better." The question will
send others to self-help books. What's wrong with me? A hundred
titles at the supermarket checkout counters shout back their
impersonal, glossy answers: "You're not looking out for Number
One." "You've not learned to love." "You're overweight and
need the Scarsdale Medical Diet." "You're failing to read your

horoscope regularly." It will send some into depression then counseling, and, let us pray, eventual, renewed health. This question will send others to divorce, to endless changes of jobs and careers and to suicide.

"What's wrong with me?" It sounds like a useful question, but if you let it be the center of your life, you will find it is hideously wrong. For it can never finally be answered. Never in this life will you live without some things being wrong with you. Yet we seek, foolishly, that precise, perfect inhuman state.

Woody Allen often points to this abiding anxiety of ours. In his new book *Side Effects* he writes a story in mock-existential style. He says of his main character Cloquet:

> A feeling of nausea swept over him as he contemplated the implications of his action. This was an existential nausea, caused by his intense awareness of the contingency of life, and could not be relieved with an ordinary Alka Seltzer. What was required was an Existential Alka Seltzer—a product sold in many Left Bank drugstores. It was an enormous pill, the size of an automobile hubcap, that, dissolved in water, took away the queasy feeling induced by too much awareness of life. Cloquet had also found it helpful after eating Mexican food."[2]

What about you? Are you in need of that Existential Alka Seltzer? Have you centered your life on that false destructive question "What's wrong with me?"

There is a better question. The central, life-giving question that Jesus asks over and over comes from a very different point of view. Not "what's wrong with them?" Not "what's wrong with the system?" Not "what's wrong with me?" But, rather, "How might God's power be shown in this life?" No matter how harsh or difficult the problem, the Christian faith is centered on hope and never despair, joy and never sadness. The disciples see the man born blind and ask, "What's wrong? Who sinned, this man or his parents?" Jesus sees the man born blind and asks, "How can God's power be shown here?"

Would you be willing to change your question, to quit reciting the long list of "what's wrong?" and to begin asking the hopeful question of God's power? That's how the best decisions are made. The God we know in Jesus Christ is a miracle-working, redeeming, utterly loving God who can turn our "what's wrong?" into healed lives and new strengths. This God is a redeemer—

a redeemer of others, a redeemer of systems, a redeemer of you and me. Even today God is reaching into lives centered on the wrong questions and seeking to touch us so that we can see life anew. Could you use that touch? You'll need to ask the right question.

3

Do You Need a Second Chance?

Some time later Paul said to Barnabas, "Let us go back and visit our brothers in every town where we preached the word of the Lord, and let us find out how they are getting along." Barnabas wanted to take John Mark with them, but Paul did not think it was right to take him, because he had not stayed with them to the end of their mission, but had turned back and left them in Pamphylia. There was a sharp argument, and they separated: Barnabas took Mark and sailed off for Cyprus, while Paul chose Silas and left, commended by the believers to the care of the Lord's grace. He went through Syria and Cilicia, strengthening the churches (Acts 15:36-41, TEV).

Do you need a second chance? As I mentioned in chapter 1, one of the problems in facing a major decision is paralysis: the decision seems so vast and important—and so final and irreversible—that we freeze and are unable to move forward or backward for a time. One reason for this perhaps, is that we expect far too much of ourselves and rely far too little on God's strength and support. A corollary reason is that we misestimate the decision, making it even more important than it is and convincing ourselves that we have to get it exactly right the first time—that no second chance will be possible.

Most important decisions *are not* made perfectly and finally in one huge motion and one smooth follow-through. Good decisions, whether about marriage or career or what have you, require continuing adjustment, tuning, and reaffirming. That is, they require second, third, even fourth chances. What's needed in life is not so much getting every decision right the first time as learning to discover and use wisely the second chance God gives.

Alan Arkin is a well-known actor who has risen to the top of his profession. In his book *Halfway Through the Door* he writes about his life after he reached the top, after he became the star that he is today. Arkin was successful, but he wasn't happy. A familiar story. How many of us have reached the goals we set but found a certain emptiness inside them? That's what Arkin says about himself. He was getting the parts he wanted. He could buy anything he could possibly dream of because he was making quite a lot of money. He was happy with his marriage. He had meaningful work in a profession that he loved. Yet there was a nagging kind of emptiness.

His gardener, it turned out, was a devout Buddhist, a real believer, one who had grown up in the East and was steeped in its tradition. He talked to Arkin about religion. That conversation changed Arkin's life. He began to talk regularly with this man whom he employed, and as he talked with the gardener, their relationship changed. Arkin's gardener became his guru, guiding him and his wife into a changed life. They changed the way they lived, the way they spent their money, the way they thought about their time. It led to a breakthrough for Arkin who now says that until that change, he had thought that the best one could do was to make some sort of uneasy peace with life. Consequently, he had believed it was best not to aspire to happiness but to aspire to coping, to getting through day by day. What he found in this new religion, in Buddhism, was that happiness was possible in ways that he had not known before. He found a second chance.

A Tradition of Second Chances

Christianity, even more than Buddhism, is a religion, a story, of a God who offers second chances. Think of the many characters of the Bible for whom that issue was central to the story: the prodigal son, that great story of a person getting a new start; or Jonah, who tried to run away from God but found he couldn't. God *forced* a second chance on Jonah. Sarah, Abraham's wife, laughed at God's promise that she would bear a son in her old age, and yet the son came. Paul on the road to Damascus—Paul, who had set his mind completely against the possibilities of any truth in the gospel, who had set his whole life toward persecuting Christians—he, too, got a new chance. On his way to Damascus he was knocked to the ground, had his life turned around, and was given a second chance—a second chance that changed the world. Peter said over and over that he would never betray Jesus and then, you know the story, when the chips were down, Peter was nowhere to be found. He ran out on his Master, but it was ultimately Peter who began the church. Scripture has many characters who were given second chances.

A second chance. Over and over the gospel is a story of people given second chances. The Scripture that accompanies this chapter is not a terribly well-known passage, but it is a significant story about a second chance. Paul and Barnabas, two of the great leaders of the early church, were missionaries who carried the Good News throughout the Mediterranean basin. Prime movers in this budding enterprise of God, they spread the gospel and trained new young leaders. Their habit had been to take younger men—promising, rising preachers—along with them to teach them the ropes. One whom they tried to take along was John Mark. But it didn't work out. At Pamphylia, John Mark left them on the first trip they took. Now names like Pamphylia don't mean very much to us, but in the story of Paul's journey, Pamphylia means that John Mark left before the going got tough. He left when all was going well. Was he homesick? Was he tired? He certainly wasn't in any trouble. The stop in Pamphylia came before Paul was stoned at Corinth or before anything terribly dangerous confronted the two missionaries, Paul and Barnabas. John Mark early on turned home and left. Later in the story, Paul and Barnabas were planning to take another trip. The discussion turned to the constant issue of who should go with them. "What about John Mark?" Barnabas said, "Why don't we take him?" And Paul, kind of a rigid character throughout the story, snapped back his non-negotiable "no." He said further, "He let us down once. He'd simply let us down again now that things are tougher." An argument ensued, a sharp argument, Scripture says, and these two friends parted company. Paul went his way taking Silas, but Barnabas sent for John Mark and took him along. A subsequent story indicated that this time John Mark came through. This time he did not turn back even in the face of difficulty. He got his second chance, and, because of it, the gospel laid hold of him and made a difference.

So please understand that you and I are part of a tradition that gives second chances and third and fourth and fifteenth and twentieth chances to those who need them. Do you need a second chance somewhere in your life even today?

Questions That Give Guidance

In chapter 2, I pointed to questions that got in the way of a good decision. Here, I wish to offer four questions that can help us move toward a second chance if we need one. It's one thing to say that Christianity offers a second, third, and a fourth chance. It's another to lay hold of that truth for our lives and let it be real for us. Such is the practical task of being a Christian. We're not called to be Christians at some ideal level, merely believing that Christianity promises a second chance. We're called to put that belief to work in us and in our hearts, in our hands and in our lives. How can we lay claim to that second chance?

The Need to Confide

First question: *Can you tell someone close about that need for a second chance?* The Bible uses the old word "covenant." A covenant describes a relationship between persons and God and between persons and other persons. This covenant is two-sided and involves telling someone else—God and other human beings—what we need. Please understand that I am not saying you should go out and bare your soul to anyone you run into on the street. That's foolishness and you will only get hurt for it. However, one of the things every one of us needs, must have, if we're to grow and to have second chances in life is someone whom we can tell. We need someone with whom we can share that deep need for a new fresh start.

Did you ever have "sleepovers" with a friend when you were eight or nine or ten years old? Those years were special and disappeared quickly. Did you ever have a friend stay overnight at your house? Perhaps your parents gave permission for you to stay up a little later than usual if you would stay in your room, and be quiet, and stay in bed. What did you and your friend do? Did you ever huddle there in bed, pulling covers up over your heads? Just you and that friend together, whispering in the dark, telling secrets that you wouldn't tell another soul— secrets about your hopes for your future, hopes that were real and rich? Did you tell how one day you'd own a ranch and raise horses? Did you tell how one day you'd grow up to be an astronaut and walk on the moon? Did you talk about how maybe you'd be a doctor and cure everyone you ever touched? Remember? We grow up and we don't talk under the covers anymore, or if we do, they put us away. Deep down in every one of us, whether we be child or adult, is a need to have someone to whom we can tell those deep secrets, those rich secrets. We all need someone to whom we can tell our need to have a new start, a second chance in life. Is there such a person for you? One of the requirements of maturity, one of the tasks that must be accomplished, is to find such a person.

The Need to Stop Pretending

A second question: *If you're looking for a second chance and need one, can you put aside pretense?* It sounds easy, but it's terribly difficult; I think all of us know that. Most of us live most of the time with a kind of cover story. Intelligence agents, or spies, have cover stories for themselves: They are doing one thing but they tell people that they are doing something else. If they are successful, if they are good as spies, their cover is never broken. A lot of us almost live that way. We go through life telling people our cover story, "I'm doing fine; things are great; it's going swimmingly." Inside, of course, we're dying. There are problems rolling through our lives, but on the surface we look wonderful. We'll never blow our cover.

Vladimir Nabokov wrote a story called "The Potato Elf." It's about a marriage, a very strange marriage between a woman who is a typical housewife and a husband who makes his living as a magician called the Potato Elf. He's a sleight-of-hand artist. The problem is that he can't leave his work at the theater. He comes home and at the dinner table makes the eggs disappear when his wife serves them, or switches the salt and pepper without her seeing because his hands are quick. His infuriating prankster habit of making things disappear on a regular basis and then making them reappear just after his wife has started looking for them frustrates her continuously.

The magician begins work on a special act. He's always admired Houdini; so the Potato Elf decides to master breath control so that he will appear to be dead whenever he wishes. He trains himself to slow down his breathing and his metabolism so that a casual observer or even someone who would come and touch him will think he is no longer alive. After he masters the trick, he puts it into his act. It's a great success, but the Potato Elf can't leave pretense at the theater. He decides one day to try his new trick on his wife. It's been successful at the theater; what will *she* do, he wonders. From their bedroom he calls to her as if it's an emergency. Then he slumps onto the bed. When she comes into the room, sees him fallen and lifeless, she screams and rushes to him. She's sure he's had a heart attack or stroke or something that's taken him from her. Grief-stricken and sobbing, she dashes to the phone and calls an ambulance. By now the joke is complete. The magician stands up, showing his wife that he's completely all right. She leaves him of course. He is unable to live with anything except the magician cover story that he's fashioned for himself; he lets it master his whole life, rendering him unable to live as a real husband to a real wife.

Can you put aside the pretense? If you need a second chance in life, sooner or later you'll have to learn to do that, to give up the cover story and live for real.

The Need for Guides in Life

A third question: *Whom will you choose for a hero, for a guide in life?* Discovering that his gardener knew more than he did about how to live, Alan Arkin chose him for a guru, a guide. Whom will you choose?

We live in an age when all the heroes have fallen. The great figures that once walked the earth, that peopled it and that we looked to for leadership are gone—the Churchills, the Roosevelts, the DeGaulles. Isn't there someone closer to home, nearer at hand than the great presidents or generals? Isn't there someone who could make a difference, who could give strength and guidance to you?

Two men made a dramatic difference in my life and in my choice for the pastorate. I suppose psychologists would say that these two were my mentors.

Gene Bartlett is one. Gene was the president of the seminary I attended and later was my first boss when he was pastor of the First Baptist Church of Newton in Newton Centre, Massachusetts. I started my work in the ministry as Gene's associate. Gene is a man of great integrity, intellect, and warmth who has held almost every honor a profession can bestow: president of a seminary, president of his denomination, recipient of countless honorary doctorates. For me what was marvelous was not Gene's accomplishments and honors, but his friendship and loving guidance as I began my work in the church. He trusted me very much, gave me so much freedom, even allowed me to make mistakes, some of which caused problems for him. He was and is a pastor who showed by his life that it's possible to be a deeply committed Christian and a completely honest authentic human being.

Then there is another man, named George Exley-Stieger. On the surface he is very different from Gene. George was pastor of Calvary–Saint Andrew's, a tiny, inner-city Presbyterian and Episcopal parish in Rochester, New York. The church was tucked away in a neighborhood of one-way streets. You'd drive right by and miss it if you didn't know where to look. The church had barely fifty people at its Sunday service.

George was the priest I worked with during the three years I was in seminary. He seemed the opposite of Gene Bartlett. Where Gene wrote and spoke with care and eloquence, George's words came tumbling out in a great jumble of love and energy. Where Gene was silver-haired, tall, and striking, George was balding, impish, and bouncy. Where Gene was often traveling across the country to give leadership, George was back and forth in the kitchens and meeting rooms of that racially mixed neighborhood caring for people in need. George, too, let me make many, oh so many, mistakes. Gene and George seemed so different. Although in a most essential way they were the same. Both men had been claimed by Christ and had decided to live constantly by his call. I realize today how much I owe these two. How much guidance and love they gave! My decision for the ministry could not have been made without both of them.

Now that years have passed and some distance stands between this present time and my daily life with those two men, I realize what I saw then as perfection in them is not perfection at all. They have flaws and I have come to know their flaws. That discovery leads to another discovery: Think of the flaws that I didn't see in myself that they must have seen! Think of all the rawness and inexperience and all the foolish, youthful enthusiasm, and yet they put up with all of it. They let me make my mistakes. They encouraged me.

How many of us have had that experience? In our coming to

maturity there were those who stood by us—not because they saw we had what it takes, not because they believed we had everything together in life, not because they thought we were professionals—because they loved us and saw something in us that we didn't yet see at all. They gave us one second chance after another until we stand where we are today.

Whom can you find for a guide, for a hero, someone nearby that can help you in your life?

The Need to Forgive Ourselves

A fourth question: *If you need a second chance, are you willing to give one to yourself?* One of the most difficult things is to forgive ourselves, to go on from our mistakes and to realize that we can start over. Sometimes we are our own harshest critics. Others stand ready, perfectly willing, to let us try again. We hold back because we think somehow we've betrayed our ideal. We can't get moving again.

Look at that story in the Bible once more. Barnabas and Paul argued it out. Finally Barnabas left Paul and asked John Mark to come with him again. Now, put yourself in John Mark's shoes. He had a major decision to make. Although Scripture doesn't say, it has to be true that John Mark said, "Yes, I'll go." Why would he say yes? His own experience demonstrated that he couldn't do it. He had chickened out once before. He had turned for home before anything had gotten difficult. Barnabas came and asked and John Mark decided to take that second chance.

Is there a place in your life where in your hands is your turn to make the decision, to say yes to that second chance that someone, maybe God, may be offering you? Do you need a second chance? Where do you need to give it to yourself?

Second Chances Call for Faithful Tenacity

Second chances are a part of what the gospel is about. We have to say yes to them when they come or else they will not change our lives. I used to know a family named Henson. I spent, I can't say how many hours with them during my years as their pastor. Often the hours were late at night. Many times the hours were in a courtroom. Their son Roger, a young man of fifteen, was a problem, a serious problem: He was a criminal. He was a thief. Over and over again he was arrested. He stole from stores in the community. He stole from the church. He stole from his parents. He stole from neighbors, usually things he could sell, such as stereos and electronic equipment. Roger was forever breaking in and then doing dumb things, not even trying to get away with it but bringing the things that he'd stolen back to his parents' home and hiding them in the garage. Everyone on the block knew where to look when something was missing from a house. They went to Roger's and then called the police. Of course, the police, as they will be with young men, were gracious at first. They were forgiving. The judge was forgiving—at first. Many times I stood there in the courtroom with Roger Henson and his mother, Mary, and his father, Les, and the judge said, "I am remanding Roger to your custody, Mr. and Mrs. Henson. Let's see if he can do better this time."

He never did better. He only did worse. The last time I saw him I had been at the church and was called by his mother. Could I come right away? I hurried over to the Hensons' house. The police were there and Roger was again under arrest. He was seated in the back of the police cruiser behind that screen that separates the police in the front seat from the person arrested in the back. His hands were cuffed. They were driving him away, off to the jail or the court. Roger smiled his far-too-confident smile and waved in that two-handed way that handcuffs force on a prisoner. Shortly after that Roger was put in jail for a bit; a month or two later I moved away from that community. I didn't hear anything about Roger Henson for about four or five years. Then one day, out of the blue, the newsletter from my former church came. It said that Roger Henson was on the dean's list at college. My mouth dropped open. Was this the same Roger Henson?

Last summer, I worshiped at that church and Roger Henson was there. A college graduate, he has a job and is doing well. Crime is not a part of his life anymore. His parents, Les and Mary, stuck with him through thick and thin, and after years of frustration, it paid off.

I tell that story because there are some of us who need to hear stories like this. We cannot always see the consequences of our giving a second chance to those who need it. If you had asked me what I would have predicted for Roger Henson some years ago, my prediction would have been that he'd be in jail to this day, or dead somewhere. Second chances often make our predictions very wrong, as mine would have been.

We have Halls of Fame all over this country. There's one in Canton, Ohio, for football; there's one in Springfield, Massachusetts, for basketball; there's one in Cooperstown, New York, for baseball. We have Halls of Fame for all sorts of sports, and we're forever electing aging athletes to these institutions. Speeches are made in their honor as we give them awards. If it were up to me to make the decisions, I would have a different sort of Hall of Fame. I would have a Hall of Fame for those who had given and those who had received second and third and thirteenth chances. This hall would be huge, and it would be filled mostly with the names of those who had made it against all the odds. I would have a section dedicated especially to those who had been arrested or imprisoned and who later, when they were released, straightened out their lives and didn't go back. I would set aside an entire wall for recovering alcoholics, who'd been up against a devastating disease, who'd hit bottom, but who'd climbed back out. I'd set aside one whole building for teenagers because every teenager needs at least a hundred second chances.

Then, at the center of this vast complex would be the Perseverance Pavilion. That would be the place where we would honor parents of adolescents. You can bet that there would be in that great hall a special plaque with pictures of Mary and Les Henson, Roger's parents. There, too, we'd honor many others who stood by those who needed it, who gave second chances until those chances finally took hold, the gospel came true, and God laid hold of that life and put it to use.

Do you need a second chance? Having a second chance is what the Christian faith is about.

4

A Word to the Weary

In the meantime the disciples were begging Jesus, "Teacher, have something to eat!" but he answered, "I have food to eat that you know nothing about." So the disciples started asking among themselves, "Could somebody have brought him food?" "My food," Jesus said to them, "is to obey the will of the one who sent me and to finish the work he gave me to do. You have a saying, 'Four more months and then the harvest.' But I tell you, take a good look at the fields; the crops are now ripe and ready to be harvested! The man who reaps the harvest is being paid and gathers the crops for eternal life; so the man who plants and the man who reaps will be glad together. For the saying is true, 'One man plants, another man reaps.' I have sent you to reap a harvest in a field where you did not work; others worked there, and you profit from their work." Many of the Samaritans in that town believed in Jesus because the woman had said, "He told me everything I have ever done." So when the Samaritans came to him, they begged him to stay with them, and Jesus stayed there two days. Many more believed because of his message, and they told the woman, "We believe now, not because of what you said, but because we ourselves have heard him, and we know that he really is the Savior of the world" (John 4:31-42, TEV).

In review, to make the best decision, we must face the issue before us. We must also put aside damning dead-end questions and ask the right question until an answer comes. We need to look for those second, third, and fourteenth chances God gives.

How do you do all these things when you're exhausted? Make no mistake, exhaustion is an all-too-common condition of everyday life. It is, in fact, a particular hazard to those who've lived for many months with an important decision looming over their lives. The emotional, physical, mental, and spiritual strain of that lingering uncertainty can drain all our reserves and leave us too weary to move. We find ourselves tired in ways sleep can't touch, that a day off won't relieve, and that a vacation won't solve. What can we do when that sort of weariness sets in?

In 1863, as the Civil War raged and the end of the fighting was far in the future, Abraham Lincoln was returning from a horseback ride with his friend and aide Noah Brooks. Brooks, noticing the president's obvious fatigue, suggested that Lincoln take a brief rest when they got back to the White House. Lincoln replied, "Rest. I don't know about 'the rest' as you call it. I suppose it's good for the body, but the tired part of me is *inside* and out of reach."[1]

That's the sort of weariness I'm talking about, the kind Lincoln knew, the kind that is "inside and out of reach." Has that sort of exhaustion laid hold of you? Are you weary in that precise way? We can understand the internal fatigue in Lincoln, I suppose. How could he have been anything but exhausted: hundreds of thousands of lives hung on his decisions, a nation's future lay on his shoulders, the end of or the perpetuation of slavery stood before him. How could such colossal burdens lead to anything but exhaustion?

We can understand Lincoln's weariness, for he bore larger than human responsibilities. It is harder to understand our own tiredness, for most of us carry no such weighty tasks. Perhaps, though, this is not so much a puzzle as a clue. Is the weariness we feel the consequence not of carrying more than humans can carry, but the result of living under too small expectations, tinier than human responsibilities, tasks that don't tire us but trivialize and belittle?

Susan Sontag, in her collection of short stories entitled *I, Etcetera*, has called one story "The Dummy." In this tale a middle-aged man who has a wife and family and who has always been the picture, the model, of stability and virtue decides he wants out. He wants out, but at first he wants not a permanent exodus but a temporary leave of absence so that he can return to home and hearth should he choose. The story is set in the future when robots have been perfected; so our hero contracts to have a robot, a dummy, made to replace him—a robot which is pro-

grammed to work efficiently at the corporation, to behave lovingly at home, to care deeply for wife and children. The day
the robot is completed, the man sends the robot home in his
place and drops out. He revels in carrying no responsibilities at
work, at home, in the community. He sits on park benches and
feeds pigeons; he stands as a silent observer on street corners;
he rides the subway and drinks wine.

Meanwhile the man's family and boss are quite happy. The
robot is both more loving and more efficient than our hero ever
was. There is only one flaw—the robot, programmed for truth
and honesty, is finally not able to keep up the charade. He seeks
out the man and tells him that he, the robot, is going to destroy
himself unless the man returns to his responsibilities—to wife,
children, job, life. Our hero then muses:

> I discovered that I am tired of being a person. Not just tired of
> being the person I was, but any person at all. I like watching
> people, but I don't like talking to them, dealing with them, pleasing
> them, or offending them. I even don't like talking to the dummy.
> I am tired. I would like to be a mountain, a tree, a stone. If I am
> to continue as a person, the life of the solitary derelict is the only
> one tolerable. So you will see that it is quite out of the question
> that I should allow the dummy to destroy himself, and have to
> take his place and live my old life again.[2]

The story ends with the man continuing as a derelict and the
robot continuing to cover for him—the robot has also been
programmed for sympathy and can't bring itself to inflict pain
on the man's family.

Do you hear what this character says: "I am tired of being a
person, not just tired of being the person I was, but any person
at all"? That's the sort of weariness that is increasingly common
in our age. A deadly, life-sapping exhaustion lays hold of us
not because we have been worked too hard but because we
have given ourselves wholeheartedly and uncritically to tasks
and goals and hopes too small to make us fully human.

We were created in God's own image, but it is not enough to
please us. We would rather look like Robert Redford or Jane
Fonda. We have been given the grandest of promises—that we
are loved and cared for and granted eternal life—but for the
most part we'd prefer a better job or at least a raise in pay. We
have been told most explicitly and simply what we're here for—
namely, to love one another—yet we cast about endlessly seek-

ing some other, better, easier purpose for our lives. We give
ourselves to purposes smaller than we were made for and we
are shocked and disappointed when we find that we are only
wearied by their accomplishment.

It was to turn us from this futility and these wearying pursuits
that Christ came, taught, died, and rose. One central purpose
of his ministry was to show us quite explicitly how to be human
beings—how to rise to the proper purposes and hopes which
will allow us to live with abundant, renewable, dependable
energy. He was, in short, a word to the weary.

Look at the passage from John 4, which begins this chapter.
This familiar story is an excerpt from the longer story of Jesus'
encounter with the woman at the well. This woman had had
five husbands and was now living, unmarried, with yet another
man. She was an outcast, a reproach, a local joke, and for this
reason she came out to the well to draw water in the heat of
the day. The custom of the other women in her village was the
same as the custom today in the Middle East—to draw water in
the morning or the evening when it was cool and, hence, less
tiring. So the woman assumed the place would be empty of
people when she came. Instead, she found herself alone with
Jesus. He had seated himself there, at the well, physically tired
from his recent travels from Judea to Galilee. His disciples had
left for the moment to buy something to eat.

The Word of Gentleness

The encounter between Jesus and this sad, confused Samaritan woman shows us the first word that Jesus offers to all who
are weary: gentleness. *Gentleness.* To a woman who had learned
to expect nothing but the taunts and abuse of her neighbors and
who had grown weary not of her work but of herself, her life,
her endless and painful mistakes, Jesus offered not rebuke but
his gentle presence. The first word Christ speaks to all of us
who are weary is a word of gentleness and acceptance, a healing
word. Do you need to hear it? Do you need to learn to give it
to others near you?

Have you heard of a heart monitor? It's an instrument car-
diologists use to see how a person's heart is functioning. Mon-
itors come in versions so small and portable that if you need
your heart checked, you can wear one for twenty-four hours.
Wearing it gives a record of how the heart functions at different

times of day and during different activities. It's a very useful tool in diagnosis.

In my imagination I picture another type of monitor that those of us who are weary might wear: a hurt monitor that could gauge and record the unnecessary pain we endure or inflict during a twenty-four-hour period. Such a machine could mark those times when what we need to give or to get is gentleness and love, but what we give or get instead is abuse, sarcasm, and indifference.

The weary ones of this world are those most in need of giving and receiving God's gentle touch. If that's your need, the irony is that you'll have to start by giving; you can't wait until gentleness is given to you. More than that, you'll have to start with those closest to you, the ones you love the most and hurt the most—the ones who love you the most—husband, wife, mother, father, daughter, son, sister, brother, neighbor, boss, colleague, employer, friend.

Frederick Buechner has written a fine short autobiography called *The Sacred Journey*. In it he tells of a time when he was six years old and his grandmother, whom he called Naya, came for a visit. Buechner loved her, worshiped her, and as a token of his love he prepared a feast for her. He writes:

> All I could find in the icebox that seemed suitable were some cold string beans that had seen better days with the butter on them long since gone to wax, and they were what I brought out to her. . . . I do not remember what she said then exactly, but it was an aside spoken to my parents or whatever grownups happened to be around to the effect that she did not usually eat much at three o'clock in the afternoon, whatever it was, let alone the cold string beans of another age, but that she would see what she could do for propriety's sake. Whatever it was, she said it dryly, wittily, the way she said everything, never dreaming for a moment that I would either hear or understand. But I did hear, and what I came to understand for the first time in my life . . . was that the people who love you have two sides to them. One is the side they love you back with, and the other is the side that, even when they do not mean to, they can sting you with like a wasp.[3]

Have you found out that truth too many times? Have you felt and suffered from the sting that can come from those who love you, and have you felt it until you've grown weary and exhausted? Our only hope is to learn the lesson of gentleness that Jesus taught by word and by example. Where can you and I become more gentle, caring, sensitive, in our daily life and work? Becoming so is the beginning of renewing strength and joy in others and, indirectly, in ourselves.

Look again at the Scripture passage. After Jesus had talked gently with the Samaritan woman and the disciples had returned, the disciples raised their very practical concern: Jesus should have something to eat. He was tired from the travel; so it stands to reason that he must be hungry as well. The disciples had, in fact, been in town buying food not only because they were hungry, but because they thought Jesus would be, too. Now they said to him, "Teacher, have something to eat." Jesus answered, "I have food to eat that you know nothing about." The disciples indeed didn't understand his words and began questioning one another. Had someone brought Jesus food while they were away? But Jesus explained, "My food is to do the will of him who sent me and finish the work he gave me to do." In his reply are two more words to the weary.

The Word of Enactment

Jesus spoke the words directly in answer to his disciples' assumption that he was tired and in need of food and strength. Jesus' response told of a deeper, steadier, more enduring source of strength—*"doing the will of him who sent me"* and *"finishing the work he gave me to do."* Are these words you need to hear?

"Doing the will of him who sent me" is an interesting, instructive phrase not exactly typical of Jesus. Normally, we'd expect him to say "doing the will of my father," but here he emphasizes "the one who sent me." Our belief as Christians is that every one of us can say that phrase, for we, too, have been sent—commissioned, fashioned, and dispatched—into the world for a purpose, and that purpose is active rather than passive—to do the will of the sender, not merely to be here simply for and by ourselves.

The Christian claim is that one way in which strength is renewed and weariness is defeated is by aligning ourselves with the great purposes of God, the one who made and sent us. The Christian claim is that to do this is to receive the spiritual equivalent of bread, meat, food. How shall we do this? How, for instance, shall we know what we are sent for and which purpose God has for us? We need one another to answer that; we need to know and be known, to love and be loved. We need a church, a community of others who also know they are sent for active duty on God's behalf and are seeking to know God's will.

We need one another, for while we are sent for a purpose, we are also a mystery and a riddle to ourselves. It is as if we, every one of us, were bottles cast into a vast and universal ocean, bottles with messages inside, messages which must be delivered and read. First the bottles must be found, recognized for what they are, handled tenderly, carefully, finally opened and the messages read and welcomed. That's what churches at their best can be. That's what I believe we can be for one another—a family of beachcombers lovingly receiving and tenderly opening the bottles that God washes up on our shore; reading our meanings and messages to one another; and bringing sense, peace, and strength to lives that have been lost in chaos and weariness.

"To do the will of him who sent me" can, I admit, sound ponderous, pious, and difficult. We preachers and theologians have talked so much about God's will that we've made it seem increasingly arcane and inaccessible. The fact is and the message of Jesus is that God's will is very close to every one of us—not mysterious or far off—but close at hand and quite straightforward. We are more likely to grasp and understand it by simple trust than we are by endless analysis, head scratching and hand wringing.

Carl Sandburg, famous writer and poet, got his start as a newspaper sportswriter. He tells of a time in 1928 when he was interviewing Babe Ruth for the *Chicago Daily News.* Sandburg asked, "'People come and ask what's your system for hitting home runs—that so?' 'Yes,' said the Babe, 'and all I can tell them is I pick a good one and sock it. I get back to the dugout and they ask me what it was I hit, and I tell 'em I don't know except it looked good.'"[4]

The Babe had no complicated formula for hitting homers. He was in tune with the game and the home runs came. It is the same for those who would follow God's will. No complicated system can explain it to you, but "tuning yourself in" through love, trust and gentleness can make doing God's will seem the most natural and life-giving act in the world.

The Word of Completion

"My food," Jesus said, "is to do the will of him who sent me and *to finish the work he gave me to do*" (italics added). "To finish the work" is a phrase, an idea, that is often part of Jesus' speech and thought. The Greek word for "finish" is *teleo* and it means to finish, complete, accomplish, perfect, do in entirety. (It is the word that is present in that otherwise puzzling statement of Jesus, "You must be perfect even as your heavenly Father is perfect." A correct translation is: "You must be complete/whole even as your heavenly Father is complete/whole.") Christ's claim is that to accomplish God's work is not to grow tired, but rather, to gain strength and energy. His word to the weary is, then, partly a question. Where have you left off the task that needs doing in your life? What have you avoided or left half-done? These unfinished works can be the source of much anguish, the reason for much weariness, the continuing cause of unnecessary pain.

Aram Saroyan has written a fine short book about his father, William, entitled *Last Rites: The Death of William Saroyan*. William Saroyan was a novelist and playwright of great fame and reputation. He died in the spring of 1982. Aram and his father had not been close for years. Worse than that, they had been deeply embittered toward one another. Aram's father was a terribly self-centered man who had little ability, if any, to show love or concern for his children. When Aram learned that his father was dying of cancer, he had not seen or spoken to him for several years. Aram Saroyan's book chronicles the long and painful journey toward reunion and reconciliation that took place in the last months of his father's life.

Because of the barriers the son and father had erected between themselves, the effort at reconciliation was profoundly difficult. At first his father refused to allow Aram to visit him in the hospital. But finally he consented to a visit, because his son promised to bring the beautiful eight-year-old granddaughter whom William so much enjoyed.

Aram and his daughter drove to the hospital and were led into his father's room. Cancer had done its awful work and the large, vital man Aram remembered was now painfully diminished—only the voice remained firm and strong. The visit was a short, quiet one. William held his granddaughter's hand. Aram thought that really nothing was being changed by his being with his father. Then as Aram and his daughter prepared to leave, the girl bent over and kissed her grandfather on the forehead.

Not having anticipated this but feeling he must do something, Aram awkwardly bent down and did the same.

Aram Saroyan writes,

> And then without hesitation, he flung his arm over my shoulder as I leaned over him, and the kiss turned into a hug. Suddenly I found myself holding my dying father. How light he was! And instead of feeling the density of muscle at the back of his neck, as I had known it all my life, it was soft there, the flesh relaxed to my hand. In that moment, he seemed to surrender and almost to melt into me as I held him. . . .
>
> "Thank you, Aram," he said, his voice deep with emotion, the long-withheld words suddenly real now on the air.
>
> "Thank *you*, Pop," I answered feeling my own emotion swell. . . .
>
> "It's the most beautiful time of my life . . . and death!"
>
> "For me, too, Pop," I answered, now literally crying.[5]

Aram Saroyan discovered almost too late that there are tasks and deeds which must be accomplished, completed, fulfilled, finished. He and his father, somehow with God's help, managed to finish the task that had to be completed. In the process, both men were freed from the terribly draining weariness that had poisoned their lives for years.

Are there tasks unfinished in your life, O weary one? The renewal cannot come until you complete the work God gives you.

Jesus' disciples knowing he was tired and hungry pressed him, "Teacher, have something to eat." Jesus answered, "I have food to eat that you know nothing about . . . my food is to do the will of him who sent me and to finish the work he gave me to do."

Resources Christians Can Count On at Times of Decision

On Being Drawn Toward God

"Do not think that I have come to do away with the Law of Moses and the teachings of the prophets. I have not come to do away with them, but to make their teachings come true. Remember that as long as heaven and earth last, not the least point nor the smallest detail of the Law will be done away with—not until the end of all things. So then, whoever disobeys even the least important of the commandments and teaches others to do the same, will be least in the Kingdom of heaven. On the other hand, whoever obeys the law and teaches others to do the same, will be great in the Kingdom of heaven. I tell you, then, that you will be able to enter the Kingdom of heaven only if you are more faithful than the teachers of the Law and the Pharisees in doing what God requires" (Matthew 5:17-20, TEV).

Perhaps the most important truth to remember at any time of decision is this: God has already placed great resources of strength and hope in our hands. This is a theme I touched on in the first chapter and now wish to explore in more detail in the pages ahead.

The picture reproduced at the top of the next page was done by an ancestor of mine—and an ancestor of yours, too, for that matter. The drawing was discovered in a cave in Niaux in the Pyrenees. It dates from the upper Paleolithic period. In other words, it is between fifteen thousand and thirty thousand years old and comes from the very dawn of recorded human culture. It is, of course, a picture of a bison, one of the animals which our ancestors hunted for food. One of the motivations for painting such a picture by our forebears was undoubtedly the desire to gain power over the creature, to insure the success of the hunt. There is something more here as well—a sense of rever-

55

THE BETTMANN ARCHIVE, INC.

ence, of awe, a perception of the holiness of life, perhaps even a reluctance at the necessity of ending the bison's life so that human life could go on.

In short, there is a spiritual sensitivity at work here. Though the human who drew this picture lived at least fifteen millenia before us, at least eleven millenia before Moses, at least twelve millenia before David and at least thirteen millenia before Christ he or she was by nature drawn toward God. It was not the mere necessity of food and desire for a successful hunt which led early humans to paint on the walls of caves. It was a spiritual need to go beyond the daily human necessities, to reach for more than mere food and water and shelter. It was the need to touch and name, to record and transmit some understanding of the holy.

These humans of the Stone Age (who were not cave dwellers, by the way) went to great, arduous lengths to perform the acts of worship and art preserved by the cave paintings into our own time. The artist who drew this bison first gathered his paints and found a means of carrying fire with him. Then, along with others in his clan, he climbed three hundred yards up a steep mountain slope to the almost hidden cave entrance. He then walked, crawled, and wriggled more than one thousand yards into the cave itself where he and the others built a fire by which to see. There in the cramped, damp confines of the cave he sketched out this most ancient surviving expression of the human soul's need to worship. There on the cave wall by the smoky firelight, he and his kinsmen gave physical evidence that they were drawn toward God, and somehow had to answer.

To be drawn toward God is to be pushed and pulled beyond a concern for the mere physical necessities of life. It is to discover that there are unbounded spiritual necessities as well. It is to undertake, without guarantee of success, an arduous, sacred journey. The one who showed us most about God, the one in whom God himself was fully present—Jesus of Nazareth—thousands of years after this anonymous cave painter lived, taught us the same central truth.

A Central Truth

"Think not," he said, "that I have come to abolish the law and the prophets; I have not come to abolish them but to fulfil them. For truly, I say to you, till heaven and earth pass away, not an iota, not a dot, will pass from the law until all is accomplished. . . . For I tell you, unless your righteousness exceeds that of the scribes and Pharisees, you will never enter the kingdom of heaven" (Matthew 5:17-18, 20).

To be drawn toward God is to be pushed and pulled beyond the accepted religious ideas of the day. It is to reach farther. Jesus underlines this in two places in this short passage. First, he says specifically that the law is to be fulfilled; that phrase, however, can be translated more powerfully and more accurately. The Greek word for "fulfill" is *pleroo*. It does mean to fill up, but here in Matthew it means, more intensely, filled to the brim. The hope and promise of the Law, all the energetic faith that God poured out at Sinai when God freed the people from slavery is to come fully into power. The law is to be fulfilled, to be "filled to the brim" beyond even the highest expectation of the religious leaders of Jesus' day, the scribes and Pharisees. This leads to the second new emphasis of Jesus: "Unless your righteousness exceeds that of the scribes and Pharisees, you will never enter the kingdom of heaven." Exceed the scribes and

Pharisees! What an impossibly demanding standard! These were the premier keepers of the legal rules who were, by definition, unexceedable in righteousness. Jesus says, "Exceed them, go beyond them." The soul that is drawn toward God is pushed and pulled past the typical, the respectable, the high-principled religious teachings of the day toward a still deeper, more loving truth.

Men and women do not paint bisons on cave walls anymore. There are no longer scribes or Pharisees to be exceeded, or if there are, they don't go by those names today. We are still drawn toward God, still pushed and pulled toward some meaning beyond the necessities of daily life, beyond the worn and commonplace religious answers. Sometimes we who are drawn toward God are drawn into loneliness, solitude, even into the soul's dark night in the relentless nature of our need and search.

Anne Sexton, who committed suicide on October 4, 1974, was one of the poets through whom this generation will be understood. Hers was a dark vision and a harsh, grueling experience, but drawn toward God she surely was. And her witness is very much worth hearing. One way we are drawn to God is through the fearsome, haunted dark, as Anne was drawn.

The opening poem in her eighth book of poetry, entitled *The Awful Rowing Toward God*, is called "Rowing":

> A story, a story!
> (Let it go. Let it come.)
> I was stamped out like a Plymouth fender
> into this world.
> First came the crib
> with its glacial bars.
> Then dolls
> and the devotion to their plastic mouths.
> Then there was school,
> the little straight rows of chairs,
> blotting my name over and over,
> but undersea all the time,
> a stranger whose elbows wouldn't work.
> Then there was life
> with its cruel houses
> and people who seldom touched—
> though touch is all—
> but I grew,
> like a pig in a trenchcoat I grew,
> and then there were many strange apparitions,

the nagging rain, the sun turning into poison
and all of that, saws working through my heart,
but I grew, I grew,
and God was there like an island I had not rowed to,
still ignorant of Him, my arms and my legs worked,
and I grew, I grew,
I wore rubies and bought tomatoes
and now, in my middle age,
about nineteen in the head I'd say,
I am rowing, I am rowing,
though the oarlocks stick and are rusty
and the sea blinks and rolls
like a worried eyeball,
but I am rowing, I am rowing,
though the wind pushes me back
and I know that that island will not be perfect,
it will have the flaws of life,
the absurdities of the dinner table,
but there will be a door
and I will open it
and I will get rid of the rat inside of me,
the gnawing pestilential rat.
God will take it with his two hands
and embrace it. . . .
This story ends with me still rowing.[1]

Many Christians know Anne Sexton's meaning. We are drawn toward God, though we have not yet reached our destination and are still rowing. Powerfully drawn, we need to make some act of permanent, steady commitment; to mark some sign of worship indelibly on the cave wall of our lives; to go beyond the sterile, habit-shaped righteousness of the scribes and Pharisees. We are drawn toward God, still rowing, though the oarlocks are rusty, the wind against us, our elbows arthritic, and though the world tells us our destination is nonexistent.

A Yes That Needs a Stronger Yes

How shall we answer? How shall we respond to this urging, this urgency inside us? What is needed, it seems, is a more complete, more committed yes than we have yet given. We have, each one of us, somewhere or other in our lives, passively or actively, intentionally or casually said yes to God's call. We've done it, or else we would not bother with the thoughts of Christ or books like this. Yet, when we feel that continuing celestial tug, that relentless pull, it is a signal that there is more yes yet to say, that further journeying is needed.

For most of us it is as though, in saying our partial yes to God, we have become a newly created, terribly awkward creature—a kind of spiritual amphibian—trying to live gracefully in two contrary elements. We want to swim with the glide of a mackerel when we're in the water and run like gazelles on land. However, we accomplish neither. We merely splash and bounce like frogs. We want to live with glib, cocktail-party ease in the world and at the same time live like saints in the sphere of God. We accomplish neither—we discover that we are sinners, but only halfhearted ones.

How shall we say and mean and live out the more complete yes which God now requires of us? How can we evolve from our partial, amphibious commitment toward a yes that takes us into the world of the spirit, what Christ calls in the Scriptures the kingdom of heaven?

Three Movements

Three steps, three movements of the spirit can make a difference.

Celebrate the Commonplace

The first is this: Learn to *celebrate the commonplace*, to give thanks for and rejoice in the everyday. This lesson rises right up out of Jesus' life with his disciples. Read through the Gospels and see what you can see. Note the high times, but note also the everyday. Undeniably, the exalted moments of the spirit are dramatically recorded—the Sermon on the Mount, the feeding of the multitude, the transfiguration, the healings, the resurrection. But notice what weaves all this together. Over and over are the small, brief but joyful and significant reports of the everyday, the times at table together with the breaking of the bread and accompanying table talk, the journeys together through Galilee, the sabbaths in the synagogue. The Gospels are filled with the joyful, everyday presence of God.

We in this generation, however, stand in danger of completely losing that ability to enjoy and give thanks for the everyday, the routine, the commonplace. Something has changed for us. Something more than the mere pace of life threatens to steal joy from our spirits. For thousands of years before Jesus and after him, indeed right up into the last century in this country, we lived as rural people, farmers mostly. The habit was to rise early to walk or ride the team out to the field, usually in the company of neighbors. This would be the daily time to visit; there might well be a song, a psalm sung together. The work was hard; the earthly certainties were few, but there was a sense of the common life, a common hope, a joy in the commonplace.

How do we go to work today? And how shall we sing the Lord's song in a strange land? It was one thing to walk and sing together on the road from Jerusalem to Bethany two thousand years ago or on the road from Concord to Boston two hundred years ago. But now we head to work encapsulated in machines of steel and chrome and glass with windows closed against noises and fumes, and doors locked against a stranger's menace; our ears are filled with the radio's traffic reports and news of worldwide menace every fifteen minutes, and our minds are ravaged by concerns of what the day will hold.

The daily routine for many of us doesn't give life but takes it away; the commonplace doesn't tune and turn us toward the Spirit, but shuts any sense of God firmly out of our lives. What is required of us is an intentional shift, a movement in our daily lives away from those routines which drain energy and hope toward those daily activities which are renewing, life-giving, and, hence, from God.

You could start on that today. Sit down with pencil and paper. Make two simple lists. On one write down the parts of your day that are renewing and on the other list the parts that take strength and hope from you. Begin today prayerfully to ask how you can lengthen the first list and shorten the second. God is first and foremost to be known in the everyday, the commonplace. We who are drawn toward him are asked to put our lives in order according to that truth.

Celebrate the commonplace. Louise Bogan, one of the fine poets and writers of this century, learned that early. Her life was anything but blissful. Unfortunate in love, often ill, without money, she somehow rose above the problems to see life from a higher perspective. Bogan says she never has expected much for herself, but her life has been filled with gracious surprises.

I used to think that my life would be a journey from the particular

squalor which characterized the world of my childhood, to another
squalor, less clear in my mind, but nevertheless fairly particularized
in my imagination.[2]

But she reports, in her old age that, squalor and all, she's not
without celebration:

> When I see some old building—one of those terrible rooming
> houses with a milk bottle and a brown paper bag on nearly every
> windowsill—being demolished, I say to myself, in real surprise:
> "Why, I have outlasted it?"[3]

Where could the commonplace, the everyday become celebration in your life? It is a way to say yes to God, to answer the
pull we feel in our soul.

Transform Your Past

The second step is this: *transform your past*; your past, your
history, in saying yes to God will change from burden to resource, from problem to promise. How many of us live crippled,
narrow lives because we are convinced that we've been wronged,
done in, irretrievably harmed by something that happened to
us last year, last week, or twenty years ago? Our parents raised
us wrong, our spouse betrayed us, our kids didn't turn out the
way we intended, we went to the wrong school, our boss doesn't
understand us, we missed the promotion. Old wounds stay
with us to haunt our present, and because we can't or won't
move past them, we are held earthbound when we would far
rather live in God's kingdom.

The Christian claim and urging is not that you should simply
put the past behind and go on free of it. Christianity is more
radical and audacious than that. Our claim is that the past, which
seems so cruel and wasteful, is in God's hands filled with promise.

William Shirer, the great author and journalist, writes in his
autobiography, *20th Century Journey*, of a conversation he had
with his friend Grant Wood. At the time of the conversation,
1926, both men were living in Paris and neither had made a
name for himself. Shirer was working as a journalist but had
not yet published anything of consequence. (He would later
gain world acclaim for his huge work *The Rise and Fall of the Third
Reich*.) Wood was painting but had not yet found the theme and
style that would make him famous and change the direction of

American art. (Grant Wood is best known for *American Gothic*.)
The two men had long been friends. They'd both grown up in
small towns in Iowa and had known each other in school. Shirer
records the conversation this way:

> "Everything that I've done up to now was wrong," he [Wood]
> said, "and, my God, I'm halfway through my life."
>
> "You're only thirty-five," I [Shirer] said.
>
> "All those landscapes of mine of the French countryside and the
> familiar places in Paris. There's not a one that the French Impres-
> sionists didn't do a hundred times better! . . . All these years
> wasted because I thought you couldn't get started as a painter
> unless you went to Paris, and studied and painted like a French-
> man. I used to go back to Iowa and think how ugly it all was.
> Nothing to paint. And all I could think of was getting back here
> so I could find something to paint—these pretty landscapes that I
> should have known—Cezanne and Renoir and Monet and the
> others had done once and for all."

Shirer offered some lukewarm encouragement: Maybe Wood
will do well someday in Paris. But Wood plunges on:

> "Listen, Bill. I think . . . at last . . . I've learned something. At
> least, about myself. Damn it . . . I think you have to paint . . .
> what you know. And despite the years in Europe—all I really know
> is home. Iowa. The farm at Anamosa. Milking cows. Cedar Rapids.
> The typical small town, all right. Everything commonplace. Your
> neighbors, the quiet streets, the clapboard homes, the drab clothes,
> the dried-up lives, the hypocritical talk, the silly boosters, the
> poverty of culture.
>
> "Bill, I'm going home for good. And I'm going to paint those damn
> cows and barns and barnyards and cornfields and little red school-
> houses and all those pinched faces and the women in their aprons
> and the men in their overalls and the store fronts and the look of
> a field or a street in the heat of summer or when it's ten below
> and the snow piled six feet high. I'm going to do it."[4]

Do it he did. Grant Wood found that his past changed from
problem to promise, from burden to resource. We are all immensely richer for that discovery. Where does that movement
need to take place in your life? It is a means of saying yes to
God.

Discover Self-fulfillment Through Self-forgetfulness

The third step is this: *discover self-fulfillment in setting self aside*.
This is a paradox that is at the center of Christ's teaching. He

puts it this way: "If any man would come after me, let him set self aside and take up his cross and follow me. For whoever would save his life will lose it, but whoever will lose his life for my sake and for the gospel's will find it" (Mark 8:34-35, paraphrased). On the surface this sounds like the most outlandish advice in the world. How can we gain life by losing it? How can self-fulfillment come through not being concerned for self? It seems to make no sense.

But it's a truth all of us have seen in action at one time or another. Think of two situations. First remember those few people you have known who are totally self-concerned. Their own problems, wants, needs, feelings are so central, demanding, and insatiable that they're never able to reach outside themselves. Writer Gail Godwin calls such people, whose only thought is "Me! Me!" Mimis (though she adds they come in both sexes and all sizes). A characteristic of Mimis, says Ms. Godwin, is that they begin conversation by saying: "Tell me about yourself! What do you think of me?" There is no joy, no sharing, no listening, no fulfillment certainly in that sort of life. Certainly there is no fulfillment in never being able to set self aside.

But is Christ's premise true? Can setting self aside really lead to fulfillment? Consider a second situation: What happens when children are born to a marriage. Ask any parents how relentlessly and irretrievably their lives are changed. For there is something about a child that is almost coercively instructive. To hold a helpless newborn in your arms is to know that even though you've never done it very well before, now you must set self aside and care for this new life. So you do. Three A.M. feedings, colicky weekends, dirty diapers and all. Strangely, imperceptibly, something begins to happen in this setting aside—a previously unknown and completely unforeseen fulfillment and love come into life, so much so that the child, for which one lost sleep and spent money one didn't have, seems no sacrifice at all, but only reward. No demand, but only gift.

Christ's claim, though paradoxical, is true in our experience. It is setting self aside that leads toward self-fulfillment. It is a means of saying yes to God, a way of answering. Because we who are irresistibly drawn must say a deeper yes than we have said before.

Long, glacial ages ago a human whose name we do not know

risked a journey into a darkened, threatening cave to mark upon the wall a record of his soul's deep need. The need to say yes, more indelibly, more beautifully, more creatively than he had before. This ancient artist no longer lives. The same human soul that lived in him lives in us. We, too, long for that righteousness which exceeds the scribes and Pharisees. We, too, are rowing toward God. Is there a yes that needs to be said in your life?

6

Treasure in Heaven

"Do not lay up for yourselves treasures on earth, where moth and rust consume and where thieves break in and steal, but lay up for yourselves treasures in heaven, where neither moth nor rust consumes and where thieves do not break in and steal. For where your treasure is, there will your heart be also" (Matthew 6:19-21).

How do you get your bearings in a season of decision? Advice comes from every side. Often it leads only to more confusion and uncertainty. What is helpful in the middle of the confusion is some clear point of reference, some unwavering landmark that can give guidance and direction in time of change.

In his novel *Bullet Park* John Cheever creates a character named Tony Nailles. Tony, seventeen years old, is a healthy, active teenager—until his world collapses all at once. His French teacher decides that Tony has had enough chances to pass his course and apparently isn't working hard enough or taking his study time seriously. She reports this to the principal, then speaks to the football coach, and Tony's eligibility to play football is withdrawn. He loses the one activity at school that means the most to him, the one aspect of his life that makes him feel important and unique. Then in the same week, quite unexpectedly, Tony finds himself in a bitter argument with his father, which ends with his father brandishing a golf club at Tony's unprotected head. After the argument Tony goes to bed.

The next morning he doesn't get up. He simply stays in bed, though he's not physically ill. His father comes to his room and apologizes, and Tony accepts the apology. He stays in bed. He's not sick, he says. He's just a little too sad to get up. Tony's mother and father try all the predictable avenues of help. They call in the family doctor who examines Tony and pronounces him fit. Yet Tony doesn't get out of bed. They bring in a high-priced psychiatrist, who suggests that something deep in Tony's childhood must have been dangerously out of alignment. He can help, he says, but it may take years. Tony's parents send the psychiatrist on his way and Tony stays in bed. The minister visits, but to no avail.

Tony has been in bed twenty-two days when Mrs. Nailles receives in the mail a note from her cleaning lady suggesting the services of Swami Rutola, a part-time cabinetmaker and sometime faith healer, who the cleaning lady says never fails. At wits' end and ready to try anything, Tony's mother calls in the swami.

Swami Rutola comes to the house. He goes up to Tony's room, lights some sandalwood, and says to Tony: "Your mother has informed me that you were an athlete and played football. I would like you to think of me as a spiritual cheerleader." The swami then asks Tony to repeat several of his spiritual cheers. First, he has Tony experience what he calls a cheer of peace—in which Tony imagines himself on a peaceful, warm, sandy beach waiting for a friend to return. Then, he has Tony repeat the love cheer, which consists of saying the word "love" one hundred times. Finally, as Tony's parents listen downstairs, they hear the words "hope, hope, hope, hope." In a few minutes their son is out of bed and downstairs with them in the living room. He is fully dressed, face washed, hair combed, a bit wobbly on his feet from so many days in bed—but well.

He says: "I'm all better, Daddy. I'm still weak but that terrible sadness has gone. I don't feel sad anymore and the house doesn't seem to be made of cards. I feel as though I'd been dead and now I'm alive."[1] With this, refusing to accept any payment, the swami leaves.

It's only a story, a piece of fiction, but like all good fiction, it is also true. There are times when we feel more dead than alive and seasons when life has sneaked up on us, hit us from behind, and laid us low. The house we live in seems like a house of cards. The lives we lead seem twisted out of shape, beyond meaning or recognition, and that terrible almost tangible sadness which gripped Tony Nailles lays hold of us and knocks us figuratively or literally off our feet.

Has what happened to Tony ever happened to you? You feel

as if suddenly the force of gravity has grown so dangerously strong that instead of feeling at ease and at home with your strength and your weight, you feel immensely heavy and weak? Gravity is so strong that you can't push yourself out of your bed or chair; the simplest tasks in life feel as if they're being done while you wear lead boots or while you are walking up hill. Where is the swami we can call in at times like that? Who will teach us the spiritual cheers that lead us to love and hope?

Or better still, let's ask a more helpful and pertinent question: How can we stay out of that difficulty in the first place? How can we avoid sinking into the sadness which seems so much a part of modern living? There is no magic swami we can call in to teach us the healing chants of hope and love, but the Christian claim is that we can build up reserves of these great saving, spiritual resources. We can set aside deep, unfailing reservoirs of hope and love that will see us through the times of tragedy and sadness. We can, as Jesus said, "lay up for ourselves treasures in heaven, where neither moth nor rust consume, and where thieves do not break in and steal."

However, for the most part, we ignore this sound spiritual advice. For we already are busy, preoccupied, doing exactly what this Galilean warned us against—laying up treasures on earth. It is precisely that enterprise which will lead us to crippling sadness and life-wasting despair when those treasures disappear.

Disappearing Treasures

On Monday, January 18, 1982, there was an interesting article in *The New York Times* about top executives in the auto industry. As you might imagine, these men and women were feeling severe stress during a period when auto sales were plummeting and layoffs and losses were mounting. The article was an interview with two psychiatrists from Bloomfield Hills, Michigan, who have many auto executives as their clients. The doctors said,

> For the first time there is real fear among these people, who have always seen themselves as untouchable because of seniority or position (or ability). I don't think these kinds of things have hit people who are in six-figure salaries (before) . . . They are people who up until now have always felt in control of things. [But now they're discovering that their jobs and careers are in jeopardy.

And] once their job is gone they have no identity.[2]

One of the psychiatrists explained that some of her clients were so shaken that they experienced what she called the "impostor phenomenon," in which they came to believe that they were not nearly as talented and capable as their positions suggested. They felt themselves to be impostors, fakes, executive masqueraders. And they were sure they would soon be caught, exposed, unmasked.

"Do not lay up for yourselves treasures on earth, where moth and rust consume, where thieves break in and steal." Remember what the psychiatrist said about the auto executives: "Once their job is gone they have no identity." Such is the price we pay for failing to follow Christ's teaching, the price we pay for laying up treasures on earth.

Who Are You . . . Really?

Where are you laying up your treasure? Here's a simple but telling test. How do you answer the straightforward question: "Who are you?" If you're anything like I am, you don't really answer that question because that's not really what people mean when they ask it. The question behind "Who are you?" is usually "What do you do?" So when we say who we are, we usually tell our occupation: "I'm a doctor. . . . I'm a plant manager. . . . I'm a teacher . . . a secretary . . . an attorney . . . a homemaker." Very often what we do, how we earn our living, is the closest thing we have to a statement that explains and identifies us. That's why it hurts so much when someone presses that question when we're retired, or out of a job, or disabled. There's nothing we can say we "do," so we hardly can answer who we are. We mistakenly believe that all our treasure, all life's meaning is on earth.

Who are you really? Isn't there far more to that question than what you or I do? Aren't there better answers?

Who are you? "I am a child of God. Though I have wandered far from home, I am not lost to God. God is calling me even now, with a voice so warm and loving I cannot help but answer."

Who are you? "I am a dreamer of dreams. Gentle, peaceful, loving dreams that do not much resemble the world I live in when I am awake. I know it is the dreams that will become reality if I but believe enough, love enough, hope enough."

Who are you? "I am the lifeguard who has been stationed at this post. I am to help all who pass this way. I am to keep them safe from harm. It is not hard work, for they are all my family."

Who are you? "I am the mail clerk with messages from home. Forgive me; I have been indiscreet and read the messages. The word is from God and it is simply that you are loved, and needed, and missed, and welcome anytime."

Who are you? "I am the prisoner who has been released. I am the debtor who has been forgiven. I am the slave who has been set free. I am the leper who was cleansed. I am the demon-possessed man who has been made whole. I am the cripple who now can walk. I am the man who once was dead, but now lives."

Are these not better, truer, more accurate answers to the question "Who are you?"—better than the answers we so easily and casually give?

"Do not lay up for yourselves treasures on earth where moth and rust consume and where thieves break in and steal, but lay up for yourselves treasures in heaven, where neither moth nor rust consume and where thieves do not break in and steal."

Adopting a Central Purpose

How, just how shall we follow this advice of Jesus? The world is too attractive, too demanding, too distracting. We may occasionally stop and think of God's love for us and at least briefly an answering love will rise in our hearts. Most of the time our thoughts run in a hundred different directions. Most of the time our concerns and hopes and energy are not focused on matters of the spirit but on the dreary but necessary business of getting through another day without giving in to our problems. How shall we keep our focus and purpose straight?

Several years ago John F. Welch, then forty-six years old, was elected chairman of the board of the General Electric Company, the youngest chairman G.E. has had in its ninety-year history. Welch, an interesting leader, had given a considerable amount of thought to the issue of focus and purpose. He had to—G.E. is a great sprawling conglomerate that took in twenty-eight billion dollars in revenues in 1980. The corporation doesn't just do one or two or thirty-five things—it consists of 250 individual businesses each making a variety of products. Welch's concern was that in all that diversity, a person could easily lose sight of the overall direction and intent.

Welch's predecessor, Reginald Jones, had tried to solve the problem of unified direction and purpose by relying on strategic planners. He had hired a whole raft of them and set up a corporate planning department. Welch took the department apart, letting the planners go because he believed that the pressures of day-to-day changes quickly make highly detailed plans outmoded. Welch's idea instead was to hold the 250 businesses together by a central idea or standard. So he told each manager of each operation that there was one criterion for success which he would accept. "They must establish their business as No. 1 or No. 2 in their industries or achieve a marketing advantage by virtue of a decided technological edge." Welch repeats this dictum at every planning meeting, and one can easily imagine it soon appearing carved in stone at the corporate headquarters in Fairfield, Connecticut.[3]

Now, I do not praise Mr. Welch for the criterion he selected. It seems harsh and undoubtedly in some circumstances unrealistic. It's not always possible to be No. 1 or No. 2. We can't at every instant have the edge on others—though I understand why a corporate chairman must think in these terms. What I do praise Mr. Welch for is his understanding that a central idea is more valuable, more coherent, more life-giving than a detailed long-term plan. A single, clear, guiding concept is far more valuable than hundreds of rules and thousands of guidelines. And please realize that what G.E. has only recently discovered, Christians have known for ages. This notion, which may help G.E. help us live better electrically, can in a different way help Christians live better eternally.

Where Will You Give Life Away?

Christianity's central, guiding idea is this: We must decide how and where we will give our lives away. Jesus put it this way: "If any man would come after me, let him deny himself and take up his cross and follow me. For whoever would save his life will lose it; and whoever loses his life for my sake and the gospel's will save it."

The choice before us, you see, is not whether we will give life away, but how. Will we spend ourselves in love and service for Christ's sake and the gospel's, or will we give ourselves away reluctantly, grudgingly, hatefully? We often mistakenly believe that there is another alternative: that we can protect ourselves, master our fate, hoard our resources and energy; in other words, life is ours to keep. But it is Jesus who is right—whoever would save his life will lose it. In the deepest and most sensible parts of ourselves we know that statement is true. We received life as a gift. It was not earned. It did not come to us by our initiative. We do not know how long we'll have it, do we? The one thing certain is that we cannot keep it; at a time not known to us we will have to give it back. In the face of that truth, we are the worst of fools if we try to clutch and save our lives.

If we would lay up treasure in heaven, if we would build those reserves of hope and love that are the only sure and sufficient antidote to life's sad and crippling times, then we must find a way through the myriad demands and infinite distractions of life. That way has been shown to us by Christ's central idea and teaching. How will you, how will I, choose to give life away?

"Do not lay up for yourselves treasure on earth where moth and rust consume and where thieves break in and steal, but lay up for yourselves treasure in heaven, where neither moth nor rust consumes and where thieves do not break in and steal. For where your treasure is, there will your heart be also."

7

Life in Abundance vs.
the Law of Decay

"Truly, truly, I say to you, he who does not enter the sheepfold by the door but climbs in by another way, that man is a thief and a robber; but he who enters by the door is the shepherd of the sheep. To him the gatekeeper opens; the sheep hear his voice, and he calls his own sheep by name and leads them out. When he has brought out all his own, he goes before them, and the sheep follow him, for they know his voice. A stranger they will not follow, but they will flee from him, for they do not know the voice of strangers." This figure Jesus used with them, but they did not understand what he was saying to them.

So Jesus again said to them, "Truly, truly, I say to you, I am the door of the sheep. All who came before me are thieves and robbers; but the sheep did not heed them. I am the door; if any one enters by me, he will be saved, and will go in and out and find pasture. The thief comes only to steal and kill and destroy; I came that they may have life, and have it abundantly" (John 10:1-10).

Ezra Tull, a character in one of Anne Tyler's novels, had a very rugged existence. His father abandoned the family when Ezra was a small boy. The one woman he loved and to whom he was engaged jilted him and married his smooth, rich brother, Cody. Even his mother failed him, offering only discipline and venom when what Ezra needed were warmth and encouragement. Toward the end of the book, having somehow survived life's continuing disappointments and losses, Ezra states the homespun philosophy that has kept him sane and alive: "Life is a continual shoring up."[1]

Life is a continual process of shoring up. It seems that way, doesn't it? No sooner do you get one hole patched than another

75

appears. At the end of the month, with luck you pay all the bills, and the next week a new pile of bills arrives. As soon as your headache's gone, your back goes out. Life is shoring up— all the time.

I had a little bout with shoring up a few years ago. I'd just returned from vacation with my family and was feeling fine because before we'd gone, we'd painted the outside of the house, put new screens in the porch, and trimmed the yard. We returned, as I knew we would, to a house set in order. I breathed a satisfied sigh and drove in the driveway after two weeks away. I could relax; summer's work was done.

After we unpacked, I went to wash up. The drain to the sink was plugged. Not to worry! I could fix it. Right? No! Wrong!

Out came the tools, on went the work clothes. Shoring up. Surely the problem was something simple, maybe just the clean-out for the trap. No? Well, then, let's disconnect this joint; that ought to do it. Not the problem, eh? Well, maybe here. No. There? There? Soon I had a half dozen pieces of pipe on the floor in front of me.

But never say die. I borrowed a plumber's snake from a neighbor and pushed whatever was clogging the pipe about halfway to Seattle, I'd estimate. The drain was surely clear now. My task nearly completed, I artfully reassembled the drain pipe and confidently stood to test the flow. The water drained from the sink perfectly. Unfortunately, it drained directly onto the bathroom floor, which was not what I had intended. Instead of shoring up, I started caving in. Enough was enough.

In a last brave effort to solve my problem, I decided to drive to the hardware store for new gaskets and washers. These would redeem me, put matters right. It was then I found out the car wouldn't start. Looking back now, after a couple of years, I am sure it was the Lord's own doing that I'd had no Liquid Plumber in the house that night. For at that moment of frustration, I might have drunk it down to end my suffering. A day or two later, though, I finally shored it up again. I got the parts I needed and fixed things. The car is running now, and so is the drain (not on the floor). What will it be next?

The Law of Decay

The one self-evident immutable law of the universe is the Law of Decay: What is now will one day no longer be. What lives now will one day die. What works now will one day not. This law operates in every corner, cranny, and constellation of the universe. It applies to atoms and to anarchists, to moonbeams and to monkeys, to Baptists and to banjos and to bank vaults, to milkmen and milk chocolate and the Milky Way. There is no escaping it.

Oh, but how we try to do just that. The Law of Decay, the inevitability of death and loss, may apply to everyone else, but most of us harbor some fool hope that in our case an exemption will be made, a loophole found, a stay of execution granted or at least a suspended sentence.

We map out conscious strategies or follow blind impulses in our effort to escape. "Perhaps," we say to ourselves, "I can purchase some exemption." Indeed a whole array of creams, pills, pastes, and devices are on the market luring us to try to buy that escape. Field-test this yourself. Stop in at any drugstore and stroll down any of its aisles. Everywhere are talismans, totems, and voodoo potions promising to repeal the Law of Decay. Oil of Olay will preserve your skin forever—oh, your bones and organs may age like Methuselah's, but you can have the skin of a twenty-year-old till kingdom come. Geritol is available for the internal parts. It comes in pints and quarts and will one day soon surely be available in six-packs. Grecian Formula 44 promises to renew your every aging follicle. Ben Gay will restore you to the litheness of youth if you can stand the aroma. Anacin will dispel the aches of age, and Fixodent will put bite back into life. Once you've restored yourself with these concoctions, be sure to pick up some of Dr. Scholl's Air Pillow Insoles. You'll definitely need them when you decide to go out to dance the night away.

We feel decay's chilly hand upon us, and we are easy prey for those who market youth, renewal, eternal life. Of course, it is fraudulent, chasing after wind. It is only more of the continual shoring up.

Or we try another strategy to escape. If we can't buy something to renew youth and repel decay, perhaps some vital change in our lives will do this for us. Maybe a new, young spouse . . . or how about a flashy car . . . a home with a hot tub. If only we could find the right rearrangement of circumstances, surely we could slough off the old dying skin like the snake or the cicada and be renewed. We seek youth, but more often than not acquire only a recycled immaturity. We'd like to be fresh and new again, but more than likely we become only aging juveniles. My word, the pursuit of change is a fetish and an epidemic, isn't it! Today one out of every two marriages ends in divorce. The average person changes jobs every four or five years. We trade houses and communities with greater glibness and less mourning than children feel over the trading of baseball cards. We pursue change to flee from decay, but in the pursuit, something has snapped or twisted in the human character. We have lost sight of old landmarks as we scramble forever toward the new, beckoning horizon. One novelist has claimed that in our endless pursuit of change we have killed off old and necessary affections and replaced them with pernicious new ones. So in these days we find many who, though completely at ease in having casual sex with a stranger or acquaintance, would blanch at standing at their sick or dying parent's bedside and saying honestly that they loved and needed that disappearing father or mother. We run from decay, but it surrounds us and meets us on every side. Life is a continual shoring up.

Or another strategy to escape decay—one that's very popular—is making ourselves the project. We become the object of our own efforts. We can see it everywhere. We jog, lose weight, take up Transcendental Meditation, join a health club, quit smoking—there's nothing wrong with any of these things, of course; they're probably very good for us. Good, unless they become our world so that we (or more accurately "I", "me," for there is room for only one in this universe) become the center of things. We can hear that happening sometimes in the language we speak: "I feel good about me"; "I'm happy with me"; "I'm learning to like myself."

Okay, fine. Loving oneself is one-third of Christ's Great Commandment. Another third is loving God and an equal third is to love our neighbor in the same way we love ourself. But that, of course, is far messier and more demanding. Worse still, it opens the universe again from the closed circle of "me" and allows our old enemy, the Law of Decay, of loss, to slip in and pursue us. But how we try to hide—to close ourselves off inside ourselves—where death and change cannot break in and steal!

There is a sort of mental disability or mental illness, if you will, which goes with all our efforts to escape decay's grip. It's a most modern malady, and it can be compared accurately to what computer programmers call "thrashing." (You can trust me on this. I know almost as much about computers as I do about plumbing. Besides, I read a column in *Scientific American* and it sounded like the guy knew his stuff.) "Thrashing" can keep computers from getting their computing done. Here's why. Inside each computer is a scheduling algorithm, a part of the machine (of the machine's program, really) which sets priorities, i.e., decides which computing task gets done first, second, third, and so on. This scheduler also has to handle outside interruptions. For instance, the computer is performing one task, and the operator punches in new data or questions. The scheduling algorithm has to decide when to stop what the computer is doing, go on to something else, then come back to the original task. Well, by now you've guessed my point. Unless the scheduler is good and quite efficient, it's possible for the computer to interrupt itself endlessly, bouncing purposelessly from one incomplete task to another; thus, the term "thrashing."

Sound familiar? How much of our time is spent that way? Lots of it, if we've decided to flee the Law of Decay, for we then must constantly be looking over our shoulders, to our sides, and behind us to see what's gaining on us. We must constantly be revising our purposes, strategies, and methods to keep death, loss, and atrophy at bay. In the process we finally accomplish nothing or nothing significant. We lose our bearings and sometimes nearly completely lose our minds. What can we do besides thrash around? After all, if life is a continual process of shoring up, we've got to keep looking for the leaks in the dike.

The Gospel's Claim

Please note right here that the Christian faith squarely, loudly, and unequivocally confronts and denies this notion that decay is in control and that shoring up is the only possible strategy for hope. The Christian claim is that death has already been defeated, that despite death's apparent daily potency, something—or rather someone—mightier than all its damaging menace has taken charge. This claim takes two forms in the Gospels. The one form is *the announcement of Christ's resurrection and the promise to his followers of eternal life.* The claim in this form is that in the long run decay and death don't count—God's power is mightier. We will be God's eternally.

This, of course, is great, but the long run can keep us waiting quite a while. And that's why the other form is also present in Christ's life and teaching and in his church. The Gospel lesson at the opening of this chapter, particularly verse 10, makes it quite explicit: "I have come," says Christ, "in order that they might have life and have it more abundantly." We Christians believe that *Christ came not only to defeat death but also to enrich life;* to teach us to live it in abundance, fullness, and love; and to teach us to face with love and hope rather than fear and flight not only death, but the Law of Decay. "I have come that they might have life and have it more abundantly." (A still more accurate translation would be ". . . life in all its fullness," or even "life in extravagance, in surplus." The Greek word *perrisson* means abundance, excess, surplus.) For Christians the guiding principle is not decay but abundance.

So how do you and I lay hold of this abundant life which Christ offers? By spending, keeping, and receiving. Let me explain.

Spending initially involves an apparent surrender to the Law of Decay. That sounds odd, I know, but let me continue. Abundant life involves living without regard for the misguided certainties of the world. It means our saying, "Yes, decay will lay hold of me, loss will come to me, death will do its worst—all these will happen. But this is not defeat. This is part of God's larger plan and triumph. For in my aging, I am not less valuable; in the face of my losses, I am not diminished; in the final fact of my death, there is nothing eternally final. The love of God will take me through."

For Christians the practical strategy is to beat decay to the punch, to admit, "Yes, life by its very living will ultimately force me to let go of every physical, emotional, and mental strength no matter how exalted it is. So rather than have these strengths stolen from me I will, at Christ's invitation, give my life away. The strength I have I will share with others, the wisdom I have I will distribute freely, the energy I possess I will not hoard but turn loose—I will spend it as one spends a gift—for gift it was from God, and in its spending there is no loss, only gain." Where could that precise strategy move your life toward greater

abundance? Is it time for you to stop fearing and shoring up
and start spending the gifts God gave you?

How shall that abundance of which Christ speaks come into
our lives? First comes spending—spending freely the gifts God
gave. Second comes keeping—keeping the sacred, permanent
commitments which are part of every human life. Here is a word
this fickle, slippery age needs most definitely to hear. Certain
commitments are indelible and lifelong; one lets go of them only
at his or her spiritual and mental peril.

What are those commitments for you? They are not easily
listed, for they are so deeply personal that it is not possible for
one person to say which commitments another must keep. But
it is possible for us to know inwardly which are necessary for
our own lives. We cannot judge others, but we can judge and
direct ourselves. We can say fairly that very regularly the sacred
commitments are quite close to home, so near that we can reach
out and touch them. Those commitments are as near as a son
or a daughter, a father or a mother, a wife or a husband, a sister
or a brother, a cousin or a friend. The hazard in this truth is
that sometimes these commitments are so close that in our
striving and desire we look past them, gazing over the tops of
their heads as it were, as our eyes turn to larger but more distant
responsibilities out in the world.

Saul Bellow wrote a novel at the end of the 1960s entitled *Mr.
Sammler's Planet*, whose theme is the rending and the mending
of the social fabric. He describes the intense passion for justice
and equality of that decade, a decade of causes, movements,
and issues. Most of the characters in the book are, it turns out,
so committed to the large issue of the day that they have lost a
sense of the personal human scale. The meaning and needs of
individuals slip from view as such grand issues as war, poverty,
and racism are confronted. One character, Elya Gruner, the hero
of the book, insofar as there is a hero, remembers the human
scale and keeps his concern for individuals, family, and friends.
Elya is a successful dentist on Long Island. His son and daughter
loathe him and his success. They throw themselves into the
movements of the day and scorn his middle-class ways, but Elya
quietly uses his income and influence to care for family and
friends in need. Elya loves not movements but people, not
causes but individuals.

At the very end of the book Elya dies of an aneurism in the brain. His uncle is in the room at the hospital when death comes. He stays with Elya's cooling body for a few moments after the doctor and nurses have left the room and then says: "Well, Elya. Well, well, Elya." Then he prays,

> Remember, God, the soul of Elya Gruner, who, as willingly as possible and as well as he was able, and even to an intolerable point, and even in suffocation and even as death was coming was eager, even childishly perhaps (may I be forgiven for this), even with a certain servility, to do what was required of him. . . . He was aware that he must meet, and he did meet . . . the terms of his contract. The terms which, in his inmost heart, each man knows. As I know mine. As all know. For that is the truth of it—that we all know, God, that we know, that we know, we know, we know.[2]

So, the abundance of life that Christ speaks of, requires spending the gifts we've been given, keeping the contract and commitments which are indelible, and receiving. Receiving what? Nothing less than love from others—the affirmation from those nearby in church or neighborhood, in family or at work, that the Law of Decay is weak and temporary but that abundant life is strong and eternal.

I have a friend who celebrated his eightieth birthday not long ago. Being eighty, he knows what it is to face the Law of Decay. Though in good health now, illness has touched him. Though he is strong, he is not as strong as he once was. Though he is full of life and energy, he also knows their limits. I suspect that in the secret places of his heart he knows times when it seems that decay is carrying the day and abundance is rapidly losing ground. But, fortunately, this friend has several others who see the deeper truth—that decay is superficial and abundance is abiding in him.

One of these others is his granddaughter. My friend received for his eightieth birthday this poem written by his college-age granddaughter.

My Grandfather's Poem

The years are shed without effort
Said my grandfather, eighty
And undiminished.
Outside the green cottage
The lake is clear as the moon

> Carries the small tide of our words.
> The years are shed without effort,
> He said, as gentle as the ripening
> Of summer strawberries—
> Tomorrow morning, I will listen
> For the stories of the loons,
> Lifting their heads dripping with water
> Again and again "I arrive, I arrive"
> The low longing moan of their laughter.
> The years are shed without effort—
> My grandfather is new, eighty
> And undiminished.[3]

Spending, keeping, receiving: these are the abiding resources that go with us through every time of decision.

Dangers Along the Way: Pitfalls That Await the Christian Who Is Trying to Make the Best Decision

Moral Energy: Its True and False Sources

"Behold, I send you out as sheep in the midst of wolves; so be wise as serpents and innocent as doves. Beware of men; for they will deliver you up to councils, and flog you in their synagogues, and you will be dragged before governors and kings for my sake, to bear testimony before them and the Gentiles. When they deliver you up, do not be anxious how you are to speak or what you are to say; for what you are to say will be given to you in that hour; for it is not you who speak, but the Spirit of your Father speaking through you. Brother will deliver up brother to death, and the father his child, and children will rise against parents and have them put to death; and you will be hated by all for my name's sake. But he who endures to the end will be saved. When they persecute you in one town, flee to the next; for truly, I say to you, you will not have gone through all the towns of Israel, before the Son of man comes" (Matthew 10:16-23).

But we have this treasure in earthen vessels, to show that the transcendent power belongs to God and not to us. We are afflicted in every way, but not crushed; perplexed, but not driven to despair; persecuted, but not forsaken; struck down, but not destroyed; always carrying in the body the death of Jesus, so that the life of Jesus may also be manifested in our bodies. For while we live we are always being given up to death for Jesus' sake, so that the life of Jesus may be manifested in our mortal flesh. So death is at work in us, but life in you (2 Corinthians 4:7-12).

When faced with a difficult decision, we immediately realize that we very much need help, resources, and direction. A concern frequently mentioned by those facing decisions is that the moral landscape seems very confused. We know, almost instinctively at decision-making times, that we need not just strength, inspiration, and the ability to ask the right question, but a moral compass. Unfortunately, that is exactly what this age of ours seems most seriously to lack. How has this happened? What can we do about it?

In 1678 in Bedfordshire, England, an almost unknown, impoverished Baptist lay preacher, a man who made his living as a tinsmith and spent what time he could preaching the gospel, published a book that changed the course of literature and religion. The book and its author are *The Pilgrim's Progress*, John Bunyan.

While few people read the book today (and if they do, they read it more out of interest in its literary influence than out of a desire to understand the spiritual life), the book was widely read and extraordinarily influential in America and Europe in the first centuries after its publication.

Bunyan's tale about his pilgrim, Christian, is a story of every person. *Pilgrim's Progress* makes explicit the basic beliefs and ideas that men and women of the seventeenth, eighteenth, and nineteenth centuries had about life. Like Christian, the hero of the novel, they saw themselves on a long, difficult, and dangerous journey—a pilgrimage of eternal, not merely temporal, significance from the City of Destruction to the Celestial City where God's salvation awaited. Like Christian, they knew they would pass through times of trial, peril, and temptation. If they were unmindful or lacking in faith, they might be swallowed up in the Slough of Despond, turned aside at By-Path Meadow, held captive at Doubting Castle, or corrupted at Vanity Fair.

What Bunyan put into masterful narrative were not new ideas, but precisely the potent, character forming ideas already held by an entire people. At the heart of it all was an understanding of the nature of the world and the nature of God. It was the nature of the world to be dangerous, confusing, sinful, and filled with an infinite number of wrong roads to be taken. It was the nature of God to provide one single certain path that successfully negotiated the world's snares and brought the pilgrim to eternal peace. The pilgrim needed dedication, direction, grace, help, and guidance. With friends and Scripture as his aides, the dark valleys could be passed through in safety. People in Bunyan's day believed that there was a way to God and it could be known and followed. They bought and read his novel because it expressed beautifully their guiding, saving ideas.

Judging from what we buy and read and what our novelists and poets write (indeed, this is one way to judge an age), for the most part we no longer believe there is a way toward God. While our writers are as convinced as Bunyan that the world is a deadly, devilish, sinful, and dangerous place, a place with infinite pathways leading to destruction, they have let go of Bunyan's hope. They do not believe there is a way through.

A glance down the list of major writers in our time—writers such as William Styron, John Cheever, Isaac Bashevis Singer, John Updike, Bernard Malamud, Saul Bellow, and Thomas Pynchon—reveals that the most each offers in the way of hope is some barely achievable, strictly limited, and completely temporary personal happiness or satisfaction. The word "salvation" is not part of their vocabulary.

Saul Bellow's book *The Dean's December* (his first novel since receiving the Nobel prize) is a paradigm of the modern novel. It is a catalogue of largely futile choices. Like Bunyan's, it is a tale of two cities: Chicago, Illinois, and Bucharest, Rumania. Bellow's main character, Albert Corde, travels between Chicago and Bucharest and finds that both cities are dominated by violence and terror. The only difference he discovers is that Chicago's violence is the random, drug-crazed sort common in America, while the violence in Bucharest is the carefully organized kind of the communist state. Bellow's message is laced with despair. He offers hope for neither East nor West. At one point Albert Corde sums up much of the novel's theme when he says to his wife: "I imagine, sometimes, that if a film could be made of one's life, every other frame would be death. It goes so fast we're not aware of it. Destruction and resurrection in alternate beats of being, but speed makes it seem continuous."[1]

Death is everywhere and we are unaware. Herman Wouk, another major novelist of our time, writes:

> The essence of the modernist novel is . . . that the world is coming apart, that a terrible and mysterious fate is running away with it, that technology is overwhelming it, that the center does not hold, and that the sensitive man can only record this and protest against it as he goes down.[2]

Our writers are an indication, a bellwether, a litmus test of what our culture most deeply believes. The evidence is overwhelming in our day that we as a society, a people, a culture, no longer share the central belief of Christendom. Bunyan's hero, Christian, knew there was a way to God and pressed on to find it. Bellow's hero, Albert Corde, knows that whichever way he turns, death and nonsense await.

Let me make clear what I am saying here, because this is perhaps confusing. I am not saying that you or I personally do not believe in God and his salvation. We do. I am saying that our world—the world we live in every day, the world of work, of media, of art, of entertainment, of leisure—that world doesn't. And I am not saying we should punish or shun our best writers because they write the way they do. Artists reflect and interpret an age; they don't create it. Bellow and others deserve our attention. They are not writing immorally. They are telling us as powerfully as they can what they see and sense and know. We in the churches need to listen. And I am absolutely not saying that the world is without hope, without ways toward salvation. We who are Christians need to know with exactness and clarity just how deep the despair is in our time.

The tragedy and danger is that many of our contemporaries— our friends, our family members, our colleagues—have lost not only belief in God, but also the ability to believe in anything. This loss of belief which characterizes the age in which we live has led to a widespread moral paralysis, a slow and silent draining away of the moral energy and judgment required to find our own way safely in the world.

Lacking a consensus that there is a way through the danger-strewn world we live in, we give ourselves to the notion that one choice is as good as another. Everything is relative, and as a consequence we find ourselves not only unable to tell right from wrong but also unable to discern which wrongs are worse than others and which rights are more important than the rest.

Our predicament is nowhere more apparent than on any evening newscast anywhere in the country. The overwhelming, undigested way TV news comes to us parallels exactly the flattening of our moral sense, the collapsing of our moral discernment. In one half-hour interrupted by six commercials we're shown pictures of Soviet tanks in Afghanistan, peasant corpses in Guatemala, flooded towns in Ohio, a terrorist attack on an embassy in London, and the latest announcements from the Bureau of Labor Statistics. Are some of these events more significant than others? Do any of them require moral choices on our part? Should we respond in any way at all (other than buying the sponsor's product)? In the absence of a belief that there is a sensible, saving way to journey through this dangerous world, we are reduced to moral paralysis, literally disabled. We are capable of viewing the world, but not of judging results and acting to affect the world around us or even our own lives. Is it any wonder we call ourselves "the me generation"? Our personal lives are about the only area where we feel we have any ability to control or any right to judge.

Of course, being human, having a God-given soul (no matter what the world says), we sooner or later grow terribly uneasy with the unhealthy, crippling situation we find ourselves in. The desire rises in us to be something other than, better than, higher than mere viewers of events. We yearn for the moral energy and perspective which our age has lost. We begin to look for some source of moral energy, some guide which can help life have direction and meaning.

I suspect there are some reading this book who are asking, "What's my life for? What does God wish from me? How can I gain a greater sense of hope and purpose?" If those are your questions, then the Christian faith certainly has answers to give. We have been in the business of offering direction, hope, purpose, and salvation for twenty centuries, in seasons of faith like the time of John Bunyan and in generations of skepticism and disbelief like this age of ours.

False Sources

Many false sources of moral energy are available in our day. I'll mention three in particular which often present themselves under the guise of legitimate, authentic religious faith: pious hatred, armed righteousness, and arrogant Christianity.

Pious Hatred

Pious hatred is common enough. I'm sure you've seen it at work many times. Pious hatred provides moral energy and a certainty of righteousness by keeping a carefully compiled list of enemies who are to be hated as the source of all evil and corruption. A fair amount of the televised Christianity you see on Sundays provides moral energy from this source. The list of enemies varies, but the standard cast of characters usually includes homosexuals, abortionists, welfare clients, and teachers of evolution. Having people to hate really can give a sense of purpose to life. As Robert Frost has one of his characters say in a poem:

> Right's right, and the temptation to do right
> When I can hurt someone by doing it
> Has always been too much for me, it has.[3]

Pious hatred fills one with energy to go out and do right, which hurts others. It may fill the void we feel, and in that sense it can attract some who have legitimate needs for moral purpose. Yet it leaves no room for seeing one's own shortcomings and flaws. It provides no opportunity or motive for removing the beam in one's own eyes. Of course, it completely violates Christ's teaching that we are to love our enemies.

Pious hatred has its appeal, counterfeit though the appeal is. One way to test whether it's been a source of moral energy to you is to ask whether your sense of right and wrong requires you to hate certain people. If so, there's a better way.

Armed Righteousness

This perversion of religion is not really new; it was part of the Crusades centuries ago and has fueled the jihad (or holy war) in Islam. But it's clearly on the rise once more in our day. We can see it in the fanatical religious belief that the Ayatollah Khomeini has stirred in Iran. We can see armed righteousness gaining ground in some Christian communities—especially those in the Third World, such as in Latin America and Africa which have adopted Christian "liberation" theology. This theology may not have influenced our thinking in America much, but the idea that God sometimes and somehow authorizes violence as a means of freeing God's people is exactly what armed righteousness contends. Often liberation theology teaches that revolution is necessary, and God's people may sometimes need to fight and kill oppressive authorities in order to bring hope to God's people.[4]

It is an odious belief that clearly contradicts much of Christ's teaching. But it cannot be ignored, because it is a belief that is gaining influence in the worldwide church these days. Many of the pope's pronouncements on his recent trip to South America were aimed at stemming this growing movement. The World Council of Churches is presently torn by debate over the faithfulness or faithlessness of liberation theology to the gospel of Christ. Armed righteousness has its appeal because in any era of moral paralysis and lost direction, guns and bullets present to the shooters a simple, exhilarating, and deadly sense of direction and purpose. It is far simpler, easier, and clearer to decide to shoot someone in order to bring about liberation, than it is to do the arduous work of building institutions which secure liberty and abundance.

Arrogant Christianity

Again, we've all seen this force at work. It comes in many different sizes, shapes, and ideological packages. It is not the private property of liberals or fundamentalists. It is that sort of Christianity so lacking in humility, compassion, and love that it is certain it alone possesses the moral vision to save the world.

In the summer of 1982 in New Orleans, the Southern Baptists held their annual convention where they elected officers. The convention provided the occasion for a pitched battle between fundamentalists and moderates. Dr. Bailey Smith, the outgoing president of the thirteen-million-member denomination, a strict fundamentalist and a great practitioner of arrogant Christianity, set the tone for the fighting in a speech before the convention officially opened. He denounced all Christians who do not believe in the absolute inerrancy of Scripture and said, "No one in hell is glad that he went to a liberal church."[5] (How Dr. Smith surveyed the opinions of those in hell, he does not say.) This is the same man who made news just more than a year before, by announcing that "God Almighty does not hear the prayers of Jews."[6] When he makes such outrageously arrogant statements, Dr. Smith is usually not ignored, laughed at, or booed, but cheered, because arrogant Christianity, though a complete misreading of the Christian gospel, has a certain appeal in our time. It offers the feel of moral certainty in the face of the everlasting vagueness our culture offers. It's a wonderful feeling, I suppose, to know that one is absolutely, cosmically, and divinely correct and that all who disagree are eternally damned. It gives the kind of energy that can keep one hopping for weeks on end, for months, for years.

There are many false sources of moral energy available in our times. But none can surpass the potency of Christ's teachings. Neither hatred, nor violence, nor arrogance can sustain a person for a lifetime. These forces, however, may give a perverse sense of purpose or direction for a time. That's why they become particularly seductive in a confused and confusing age.

The Main-Line Churches' Inadequate Position

Dr. Leonard Sweet, a seminary friend and classmate of mine, teaches church history at Colgate Rochester/Bexley Hall/Crozer Divinity School. He recently published a fine article in *The Christian Century* entitled "Not All Cats Are Gray: Beyond Liberalism's Uncertain Faith." In it he says that main-line religion has lost its ability to affirm beliefs decisively and has often withdrawn from the responsibility of giving moral guidance into a kind of "I'm OK, you're OK" blandness. He writes:

> In the punctuation of faith, the exclamation mark of an absolute, the colon of a secure conviction, the dash of a dependable axiom, the period of a "center that holds" have been shoved aside by the supremacy of the question mark, which has come to occupy an almost iconic place in the contemporary liberal mind.[7]

One of the consequences of main-line churches enshrining the questions rather than affirming our beliefs has been the growing and strident movement on the religious right. A loose confederation of churches characterized by but not limited to the Moral Majority, have begun to press insistently for a long list of so-called "Christian issues"—prayer in school, the teaching of "creation-science," an anti-abortion amendment to the Constitution, to name only a few. It is by no means surprising that such churches should be growing, given the lack of conviction and affirmation from the main-line denominations. However, too much certainty is just as dangerous and wrong-headed as too little. A completely rigid, rule-oriented view of right and wrong is just as contrary to the gospel as the do-your-own-thing permissiveness of some parts of liberal Christianity.

What is needed from the churches in these days of moral confusion are two things: a clear affirmation of what we believe about the truths we have received and humility about our imparting those beliefs to others. Affirmation is needed because we really are heirs to the great and saving truth of God's love in Jesus Christ. Humility is required because we are still merely human and not God and, as the Scripture that opens this chapter puts it, "we have this treasure in earthen vessels." The truth we teach and believe is holy and eternal; our understanding of it is limited and subject to correction. Let us affirm it, but with humility and not arrogance.

What Guidance?

What guidance for moral decision making does Christ offer? What sources of energy rise up out of his teaching in the New Testament?

The Scripture at the beginning of this chapter shows a characteristic of the teaching of Jesus. It begins: "Behold, I send you out as sheep in the midst of wolves; so be wise as serpents and innocent as doves." Wise as serpents, innocent as doves. How can one be both wise and innocent? Both are high qualities to aspire to, but they are in some ways incompatible with one another. Gaining wisdom almost always brings with it a loss of innocence. Remaining innocent requires a naivete and lack of ambition which keep one from gaining wisdom. These two good qualities are not compatible. But this is exactly what Christ intended. It is his habit, his technique, his plan, to put his followers under tension, to set before us twin but not entirely compatible goals. He does it at other points in Scripture. He tells us to "love our neighbor"; fine, but then, he adds, "as yourself." He tells us that if we would save our life we will have to lose it. He tells us to take up his yoke *and* that his burden is light. Again and again Christ pairs seemingly conflicting choices. It is his way of giving us an inexhaustible source of moral energy and direction.

This method of teaching moral vision may sound strange at first. It isn't really. It's so natural that we hardly ever think about it. Think of the way we train children to live morally in a confusing world. Oh, I know at first thought we may say that we brought our children up (or that we ourselves were brought up) with a strict code of behavior—the rules of right and wrong. But there was more to it than that. The pairing of conflicting goals is a constant resource for training and building moral vision.

Remember the times when your child first lied to you, perhaps

about something small around the house (he or she had broken
a dish, but hid it and didn't tell you). And, of course, being a
good parent you decided it was time to work on honesty. You
had a talk with the child. "You can tell me, Son. It's important
to tell the truth even if it's unpleasant. I'll still love you even if
you've done something you're not proud of. What hurts most
is when you lie to me." It all goes wonderfully well. The lesson
is learned. The fibbing at home stops.

Three weeks later you and your family go to a neighbor's for
dinner. After the fruit salad comes the rest of the meal. When
the creamed asparagus is passed to your son and he is politely
asked, "Would you care for some?" he responds: "No. That
looks terrible. I couldn't eat that." Later that evening you explain
to him that while you appreciate his honesty, honesty is not the
only issue. There is such a thing as courtesy as well, and if he
doesn't learn to practice it pretty soon, he's going to be in honest
trouble with you.

As followers of Christ, we are given a different means of
direction than the simplistic ideas of the world. We are not given
a rigid code which is to be inflexibly applied; nor are we simply
left adrift to find our own way or do our own thing. Instead we
are given certain qualities and certain goals which are not entirely
congruent with one another, which must be held in tension. It
is by striving to serve these paired but difficult goals that we
live as Christ's disciples. Understanding this can be of immense
help to anyone in the midst of a major decision. Look with me
at three such paired, or twin, goals.

Wisdom and Innocence

Christ puts both wisdom and innocence before us as goals for
Christian moral behavior. Though these words are twenty centuries old, they could hardly be more timely and fresh, for they
strike to the center of the temptations of a scientific and technological age. That temptation is to put innocence aside, to let
it go as an immature and unrealistic value, and relentlessly to
pursue practical, immediate wisdom. The temptation is to avoid
the questions of innocence and evil and to call useful and good
only the discoveries that lead to advantage over others.

Our technological age is a continuing record of innocence cast
aside, forgotten at our peril. Albert Einstein, the genius who
reformulated the world of physics and for a time pursued wis-

dom out of the sheer and innocent joy of knowing the elegance and the structure of the universe, ultimately cast innocence aside. In his now famous letter to Franklin Delano Roosevelt, written in the midst of World War II, he suggested that an atomic weapon of immense destructive power could be built and that the United States should develop one. With that single, momentary betrayal of innocence in favor of immediate wisdom and technological capacity, the nuclear age was born. Einstein later came to regret deeply his part in the birth of the Manhattan Project. It is the nature of the universe that even a single betrayal of one of the goals which must be balanced can lead to almost unimaginable harm.

Sunday, June 27, 1982, may well be remembered one day as another significant date in which innocence was deemed unimportant in the face of military and technological wisdom. The space shuttle *Columbia* was launched that morning on its fourth and final test flight. But this flight was different from the three earlier trips. We did not hear as much of the activities of the astronauts on this launch. No television pictures of the experiments in the cargo bay were shown over home screens because this was a trip to test military equipment for use in space. Yes, space, too, begins to be filled with armaments and the possibilities of battle. What we once called the last frontier and looked on as an innocent, pristine vista to be explored, is now increasingly inhabited by the machines of war.

Make no mistake; we cannot forever compromise our innocence in favor of wisdom and power. Christ teaches that both must guide us. We require both for human survival. For innocence without wisdom is incompetent, but wisdom without innocence is brutal.

Character and Tolerance

This is a particularly vital issue for us in the church. For as an institution we are in the business of fashioning character, of shaping the guiding beliefs of children and adults. The risk in this enterprise is, on the one hand, that we can so emphasize what we believe as the truth we've received through Jesus Christ that we lose tolerance or respect for other positions. (That, it seems to me, is the great risk of fundamentalist Christianity.) On the other hand, we can so stress tolerance and respect for all other beliefs that we let go of our responsibility to say firmly, clearly, and intelligently what we believe and what sort of character we're trying to shape. (This seems to me to be the great risk of liberal churches.) What we believe and what we tolerate must be held in tension. We must know and say what we believe and to whom we're committed as Christians. At the same time we must hold those beliefs with sufficient maturity and humility that we have tolerance and respect for the diverse beliefs of others.

The tension needed between tolerance and character was one that Dag Hammarskjold learned during his hard, productive years as secretary general of the United Nations. In his role as a mediator between warring parties, he needed large doses of both. He writes in his book *Markings:*

> Lack of Character - All too easily we confuse a fear of standing up for our beliefs, a tendency to be more influenced by the convictions of others than by our own, or simply a lack of conviction with the need that the strong and mature feel to give full weight to the arguments of the other side. A game of hide-and-seek: When the Devil wishes to play on our lack of character, he calls it tolerance and when he wants to stifle our first attempts to learn tolerance, he calls it lack of character.[8]

Freedom and Equality

We're so used to hearing freedom and equality mentioned side by side that we can easily brush right past the words and say we're for both and claim there is no tension or incompatibility between the two. Tension there is, and these two dear values have been in conflict in recent years.

The sixties and early seventies were years when the cry for equality was loud and impassioned. Laws were changed and bureaucracies arose to carry forward their intent. Equal opportunity and affirmative action became part of our vocabulary. Great gains were made in the treatment of blacks, and Hispanics, and women by our society. But in the press toward equality some freedom was diminished. The government now was telling businesses, universities, and cities whom to hire and whom to promote. Freedom and equality chafed against each other. Today the pendulum swings again, with many voices emphasizing freedom. Freedom from regulation, taxation, government intrusion.

The danger in this present movement, as in the sixties and as in earlier periods in our history, is that we will resolve the tension rather than live with it. We must be committed to nothing less than both freedom and equality within our system of government. If the two values rub against one another, lead to debates and change, so much the better. This is perhaps the greatest source of moral energy the nation's founders built into the system when they wrote: "We hold these truths to be self-evident, that all men are created equal, that they are endowed by their Creator with certain unalienable Rights, that among these are Life, Liberty and the Pursuit of Happiness." Putting equality and liberty side by side as guides for future generations has provided the energy to change and grow. Yet we must preserve these two crucial values by maintaining tension between them.

In Summary

We live in an age of moral confusion. In such a time it is tempting to turn to some false certainty as a sustaining guide. Many such counterfeit sources of moral energy are available. But what is crucial for us as Christians is to remember that Christ rooted moral decision making in the tensions between twin but partially incompatible goals. Three of these tensions which can give guidance today are the tension between *innocence* and *wisdom*, the tension between *character* and *tolerance*, and the tension between *freedom* and *equality*. If we can avoid the too simple, too certain dictates of the false religions of our day, God may yet let us see a rebirth of moral energy in our country and our world.

In C.S. Lewis's *The Screwtape Letters*, the devil, Screwtape, tutoring a young friend in the art of making people immoral, explains that "nonsense in the intellect may reinforce corruption in the will." The trick, he says, is first to convince people that fashion should rule them because fashion is the "Tide of History" and hence, "progressive." Then he adds: "We direct the fashionable outcry of each generation against those vices of which it is least in danger. . . . Cruel ages are put on their guard against Sentimentality, feckless and idle ones against Respectability, lecherous ones against Puritanism. . . . "[9]

Today Screwtape, the devil, might seek to blur our moral vision by putting us on guard against complex issues and hard thinking. How? By telling us that life demands a simpler choice: "Come down on one side or the other. Collapse the tension.

Choose wisdom. Let go of innocence. Or choose innocence and let go of wisdom." Christian discipleship resists that simplistic but fashionable outcry and chooses to live under God's tension. Inexhaustible moral energy and purpose derive from precisely such a choice.

9

Half Dead Is No Way to Live

But he, desiring to justify himself, said to Jesus, "And who is my neighbor?" Jesus replied, "A man was going down from Jerusalem to Jericho, and he fell among robbers, who stripped him and beat him, and departed, leaving him half dead. Now by chance a priest was going down that road; and when he saw him he passed by on the other side. So likewise a Levite, when he came to the place and saw him, passed by on the other side. But a Samaritan, as he journeyed, came to where he was; and when he saw him he had compassion, and went to him and bound up his wounds, pouring on oil and wine; then he set him on his own beast and brought him to an inn, and took care of him. And the next day he took out two denarii and gave them to the innkeeper, saying, 'Take care of him; and whatever more you spend, I will repay you when I come back.' Which of these three, do you think, proved neighbor to the man who fell among the robbers?" He said, "The one who showed mercy on him." And Jesus said to him, "Go and do likewise" (Luke 10:29-37).

In time of decision, whether we realize it or not, we deeply need the help of others. Most especially we need the help of a loving community, that is to say, a church.

Let me relate a story about two old friends from college days—two who when they married each other were full of life and promise—who had something go wrong, terribly wrong, in their life together.

The telling, killing moment came in July of 1983. It was dusk on a warm summer Saturday night in Missouri. John Kroeger arrived home from a day of fishing with his two boys. His wife, Kathy, was not in the house when he got home, but there was no special concern in that. She often went for an evening walk in their safe, rural neighborhood. She often visited with friends.

John set about fixing dinner for himself and the boys, then bathed them and put them to bed. Sleep came quickly for both sons, for they'd been up since 5 A.M. and the fishing had worn them out with delight.

John sat down, switched on the TV, and had a beer. When he noticed his watch again, it was 9:30 and dark outside. He decided to check on Kathy. He phoned the two neighbors she was likely to visit, but they had not seen her that Saturday. He walked out on the front porch, leaving the porch light off so he could see farther in the dark. He peered down the lane that led up to their pre-Civil War farmhouse. Kathy was not in sight. He called her name. No reply.

A dark reminiscence stirred in John. He went inside, got his flashlight and walked out in back of his house. He headed for the tree line just past the garden. It was about ten yards to the left of the garden that the beam of the flashlight fell upon a gap, an indentation in the tall grass of the meadow. John knew what he would find. He walked to the spot and saw Kathy stretched out in the grass. He felt for a pulse. It was weak but steady. Her skin was cool to the touch. She did not stir when John stroked her brow or called her name.

John switched off the flashlight and stood up. Frozen in weary indecision and lost in thought, he stood there in the dark over his wife's half-dead body. After who knows how long, he turned, walked back into the house, and went upstairs to the boys' rooms. He made sure they were still asleep and all right. John went to the room he shared with his wife, and walked through into the adjoining bathroom. On the counter by the sink were the empty bottles of sleeping pills he knew he would find. John switched off the bathroom light, changed into his pajamas, turned on the air conditioner, and went to bed.

He slept soundly and woke at first light. He got the boys up, dressed them, and drove them to his parents' house so that they could go to church without him. He then returned to the farmhouse and again walked out to look at Kathy. She was still breathing, stronger and deeper now. Her pulse was not as weak this morning. As he touched her forehead, she stirred and opened one eye. John said to her, "I'll call the ambulance."

Kathy was taken to the hospital and her stomach pumped. She physically recovered. But the marriage was over—John knew it was over when he discovered himself unable to offer help to his half-dead wife when she needed it most. Kathy knew it was over when she learned that John had found her but chose to leave her till morning, to do nothing to save her, to go to sleep.

From the way I've told the story, it sounds as if John was a vicious, uncaring husband. Does it sound different when I tell you that this was the fourth time in sixteen years of marriage that John had found Kathy this way? The fourth time—but the first time that he did not immediately call the ambulance. Kathy was not the only one half dead on that July night in Missouri; John, too, was half dead with weariness from endless starting over. Something in the marriage had gone poisonously wrong, and neither John nor Kathy could finally redeem it, though they tried. They tried it all—church, counseling, new jobs, new houses, new cars, new friends. But nothing worked, and finally they each discovered that half dead is no way to live. My prayer is that beyond the pain they feel now as they divorce, they will find new hope and a future where death is not so present and powerful in each of their lives.

Half dead is no way to live. But vast numbers of us live that way. Our lives are nearly dominated by the powers of death: timidity, rage, jealousy, dissatisfaction, isolation.

A Story

Jesus tells a story with some clues hidden in it. "A man was going down from Jerusalem to Jericho, and he fell among robbers who stripped him and beat him and departed, leaving him half dead. Now, by chance a priest was going down that road; and when he saw him he passed by on the other side. So likewise a Levite when he came to the place and saw him passed by on the other side."

Let me mention two points here before we go on. First, I'd like you to see the story from the point of view of the man beaten and half dead, who presumably doesn't even clearly notice these two clergy types who pass him by. In your imagination you be the one unconscious or semiconscious by the road. Second, let me say a word about the priest and the Levite, whom we usually scorn in this story. How often, in fact, have you heard this tale told and had it pointed out that the priest and Levite were just too callous, too indifferent, too busy, or too cowardly to stop and help?

There's more to it than that. It's no accident that Jesus says the man was half dead. He's conjuring something here for his audience, an audience familiar with the laws of first-century Judaism. The laws for service in the temple were clear, and the priest and the Levite, who had special elite status at the temple in Jerusalem, knew the laws and followed them scrupulously. They were bound by their religion to keep from any contact with a corpse. In fact touching a corpse would disqualify them for service in the temple for a year. So what do they do with a man half dead? They stay clear. Even if they feel a bit of concern for him and his plight, they can't risk helping—he might die while they are touching him. Then their highest calling would be taken from them. So, please see, they do not scorn our half-dead victim out of mere busyness or callousness or indifference—but because they believe there is a higher purpose than caring for someone in need, a higher purpose than saving life.

Along comes the Samaritan, who lives outside the Jewish law, presumably indifferent to it but by no means indifferent to the human need he sees in front of him. He may not care for God's temple in Jerusalem—indeed he's not even allowed near that place lest he defile it by his "foreignness"—but he does care for life, even the life of a half-dead stranger. And he acts promptly on that care and concern. The Samaritan stops, goes to the half-dead victim, and binds up the wounds.

What Do You Need?

Remember whose eyes we're seeing this story from, the half-dead man's. Half dead is no way to live. What do you need if you're half dead? *You need someone or something that is unequivocally committed to life, someone who puts life first* before even the highest calling, before even service to God.

William Least Heat Moon is a little-known name that will become better known. He has written a marvelous, stirring book called *Blue Highways*, which sounds trivial, like a travelogue, but it isn't. It's the personal account of his 15,000-mile, year-long trip around the United States following the back roads instead of the interstates (the blue highways on the maps instead of the red ones.) It's more than a record of his travels; it's a testament to human vitality, courage, and kindness as Least Heat Moon tells of one fascinating encounter after another. It is, and deserves to be, a best-seller. I commend it to you if you want to hear a firsthand account of human grandeur and God's presence. But the book almost didn't get written. It wouldn't have been written except that something unequivocally, almost stupidly, committed to life touched William Least Heat Moon when he was half dead.

The idea for the book came in the middle of the night on February 17, 1981, a day of "cancelled expectations." It was the day William had been fired from his position as an English teacher at the University of Missouri at Columbia because enrollment was down, he was told, and he wasn't needed. It was the day that William called his wife from whom he'd been separated nine months. He called hoping to arrange a meeting to seek a reconciliation, but his wife went on and on instead about her new friend Rick. The marriage was over.

In the sleepless night that followed that hurt-filled day, the wildly improbable, distinctly irresponsible idea of driving the back roads of America in search of material for a book came to William Least Heat Moon. By morning, even though he had many fears and doubts about the project, he was committed. He started outfitting his van for the trip.

On March 19, the last night of winter, the night before his departure, he went to bed but couldn't sleep. The craziness of what he was about to do overwhelmed him. He almost was ready to give it up and withdraw into his half-life of disappointment and cancelled plans. Then as he puts it,

A strange sound interrupted my tossing. I went to the window, the cold air against my eyes. At first I saw only starlight. Then they were there. Up in the March blackness, two entwined skeins of snow and blue geese honking north, an undulating W-shaped configuration across the deep sky, white bellies glowing eerily with the reflected light from town, necks stretched northward. Then another flock pulled by who knows what out of the south to breed and remake itself. A new season. Answer: begin by following spring as they did—darkly, with neck stuck out."[1]

For Least Heat Moon, this was the touch he needed, a chill March morning filled with the honk of Samaritan geese, out unwittingly binding wounds, offering life, touching off in him this contagious instinctual trust that draws one even into the cold, unblossomed barrenness of spring in the trust that life is coming, warmth is coming, healing is coming.

Half dead is no way to live. You'll need someone or something unequivocally committed to life in order to be made whole. You'll need a Samaritan on the road, a church filled with loving people, a sky full of geese, or an indelible friendship if recovery is to come.

Have You Been Mugged?

Once someone or something touches you and offers healing, there's more, and *you'll* have to do this part: *You'll have to admit you've been mugged, "blind-sided," laid low, left half dead.* Notice the conversation that does *not* take place in the Bible story. Our Samaritan stops and helps. Our half-dead man presumably revives, but says nothing. He accepts the needed help.

Do we accept needed help when we're half dead? Oh no, of course not, or at least not without a fight. Let's say that one of us half-dead types is lying by the road, and the Samaritan stops to help. What do we say in response to his sincere, not merely casual, "How are you? Can I help?" You know what we say: "I'm fine. Don't worry about me. I just love to lie here by the road bleeding and bruised. I come out here every day just for the view. Now, don't worry about me. I'll be okay. Don't need any help! Take your wine and your oil and your beast and yourself on down the road. And have a nice day." We, in short, lie. We tell everybody we're doing fine, though spiritually and perhaps physically we're at death's door or at least on the sidewalk outside death's front gate. If we want to quit being half dead (which is no way to live, you'll recall) we will have to admit we've been mugged. Probably nobody specifically, exactly beat us up, stripped us, and left us for dead, but mugged we've been nonetheless.

It happens in quiet, nonviolent but still brutalizing ways. The love we've given and expected to receive in return for a lifetime is suddenly absent, unanswering, and our partner has run off with our entire emotional bank account while we weren't looking. Or while pressed into the crowd of colleagues and competition at the corporation we serve, we have the pocket we kept our best ideas in picked, and someone else takes credit. The promotion we've wanted never comes. Sometimes the friend, the one friend we've confided in about our deepest selves, betrays our trust. It turns out that it was a con game all along, and what's been stolen is not our wealth but our spirit, not our possessions but our self-possession, not only our confidence in that friend but also our confidence in our own judgment.

To move toward whole, full life, we have to admit where we really are and what our needs are—not, to be sure, to just anyone or everyone but certainly to those who are unequivocally committed to life, to the Samaritan that can help and heal.

But life trips us up and drains us, even if no one in particular means us ill. Have you ever seen children of six, seven, or eight offered a glass of something they dearly love—not milk, not water, but soda, or fruit drink. Brash with untested confidence, they grab a glass, grasp the pitcher or bottle, and then pour themselves a brimful portion. Next you see them trying to make their way to the table with the glass full to overflowing, but, of course, the contents are so precious they must not spill a drop. So they put both hands around the glass, focus their eyes on the rim and, shuffling rather than lifting their feet, head slowly, confidently for the dining room table. You can see it coming a mile away. It's the rug that's gonna get them. Warnings do no good; the children's senses are tuned elsewhere and down it all goes with a crash. And being children, they come up crying and flailing, weeping at their loss rather than naming their problem, cleaning the spill, and asking for a refill.

We're no different, just older. We half-dead, life-weary types carry our souls, our precious energy, in a glass before us, and we are so worried about spilling it and losing it that we can't take our eyes off the surface of self for even a moment—not even long enough to see where we're going. Here comes the first crack in the sidewalk and down we go. Being at least nominally adults, we do not come up crying, at least not on the outside. We come up bleeding internally but telling everyone, "I'm fine. Have a nice day."

Half dead is no way to live. If you want to be healed, you'll have to admit you've been mugged. If you want the cup filled again, you better tell somebody you tripped and spilled it, and it's empty now.

A Place for Recovery

You and I need a place where healing can not only begin but also continue. Jesus' parable says that after the Samaritan had bound up the half-dead man's wounds, he took him to an inn and provided for him so that the healing could continue.

Do you remember what it was like when you got sick as a

small child—not deathly sick, but slightly sick—with measles, the flu, perhaps chicken pox? At first you felt just awful as you experienced fever, chills, vomiting. It was wretched. But soon, usually, they were under control; aspirin, chicken soup, maybe some medicine brought improvement. Now you still weren't well enough to go to school, but you were well enough to enjoy your recovery.

I wonder if a church could be such a place, a place where you could, when well enough, begin to enjoy your recovery. Maybe if we changed our ritual. Maybe if we rearranged what we do to make the place more like the sickroom of childhood. I know! We'll take out the altar and put in a great bed with at least six pillows. We'll cover the bed with quilts and afghans from Grandma and have stuffed animals and dolls everywhere: Pooh and Eyore, Raggedy Ann and Raggedy Andy, Flopsy and Mopsy and Peter. We'll add two great overloaded bedside tables—one for all the books you'll read or have read to you; the other for the thermometer, the heating pad, the aspirin, the fruit juice, the vaporizer.

Once we're set up, we'll take turns playing parts, each of us getting a chance to be propped up in bed and pampered for a time till we're better and each having a chance to do the pampering. Who'd like to read the stories? Who'd like to fluff the pillows? Who wants to run to the store for ice cream? Who wants to heat the soup? I'll pop the popcorn. You make the toast.

Yes, that's it—we'll have to change the way we worship in order to make our churches places of recovery, places to get well as we got well when we were kids. Instead of robes for choir and clergy in the processional, we'll look in the catalogues and order some of those wonderful, fuzzy childhood pajamas that zip up the front and have feet at the ends of the legs. Be careful not to slip and slide when we come down the aisle for the processional!

Coming back from imagining this worship scenario, we must remember that half dead is no way to live. But the good news is that we don't have to live that way. John and Kathy never found that out, or haven't yet. No one unequivocally committed to life ever touched them, and they were always too fine to admit they'd been mugged. Then, too, they had no place to recover. May God heal them yet. And may we in Christ's churches learn to be agents of such healing.

10

Four False Commandments

"When the unclean spirit has gone out of a man, he passes through waterless places seeking rest; and finding none he says, 'I will return to my house from which I came.' And when he comes he finds it swept and put in order. Then he goes and brings seven other spirits more evil than himself, and they enter and dwell there; and the last state of that man becomes worse than the first" (Luke 11:24-26).

In several earlier chapters (particularly chapters 1, 2, and 8) I touched upon the hazards of decision making and in particular upon the seductive but ultimately misguided advice the world often pushes at us at decision-making times. In this chapter and the two which follow, I want to examine in greater detail these pitfalls and dangers.

John Lewis is approaching fifty. He is a marvelous, brilliant man. Because he is a natural leader, people are attracted to him and seek out his advice and thoughts. He is an engineer by trade as well as an inventor, using engineering in some very creative ways. He is warm and caring and has many friends. (I am fortunate to be one of them.) He's a true family man who cares much about his wife and his children. Yet in the midst of all his success John is feeling some considerable frustration now. He's full of questions. He knows that his youth is gone. He knows at the same time that his future is secure. He doesn't have to worry about where the next meal is coming from or how to provide for his children's education. These seem well under control. Yet there is in him a sense that something, somewhere, went wrong.

What is it? Well, certainly we can immediately say that John Lewis is going through a mid-life crisis. We've heard it over and over. There's ample literature. We can't walk through the su-

permarket without seeing by the checkout stand a magazine
emblazoned with an article title that tells us how to find out if
we're going through a mid-life crisis.

Yes, John is going through one; that's certain. All of us seem
to go through them. In fact, if you reach forty, forty-five, or
fifty, particularly if you are a man, and you haven't had a mid-
life crisis, you feel rather cheated. It's a great excuse, after all,
to do all those things that you wanted to do but which convention kept you from doing. That's why so many men in the forty-
to-fifty age range buy convertibles. They buy them then drive
around with the tops down until the bald spots on the back of
their heads are fried to a crisp. Or they join the health clubs
and try to sweat off the pounds until they can get into bathing
suits that they wore when they were nineteen. You can tell these
types easily by their wizened, yet somehow adolescent, look.

Mid-life crisis certainly is what John Lewis is going through,
but in John's case as with most mid-life crises, more is involved
than a change of life. John's disappointment with his work didn't
and doesn't now stem simply from his sense that he will not
rise much farther. Indeed John's success has been formidable.
He does not live with a sense that he's been passed over or
denied opportunity. To the contrary, he has been offered pro-
motions time after time. However, there's been an impulse in
John—something that was born out of his very Christian commitment—that led him to turn down each opportunity presented. Each time someone for whom he worked offered him a
promotion, John let it go by, saying it wasn't for him. He has
said, "No." He's done it enough so that at this point his su-
pervisors have simply quit coming to him. They've made the
conclusion that John doesn't want those kinds of opportunities
anymore.

When John said no to those opportunities offered him, he did
so not out of laziness or lack of drive or mere timidity. He said
no because of his Christian commitment. There was something
in John's understanding of the gospel that led him to decline
positions of authority or power over others. Call it humility. Call
it a servant attitude. Call it what you will, it was so strong in
John that he literally felt it sinful to consider promotion. To be
sure, John is questioning those decisions now. He's wondering
whether he did the right thing, even wondering if he might not

have served God better by saying yes instead of no to the opportunities offered. It's too late now; there will be no more opportunities offered, and John knows it.

So John is undergoing not just a mid-life crisis but also a crisis in faith. As you can see, the crisis is directly rooted in his sense that he may have made the wrong decision. He wonders what his Christianity really ought to mean and ought to be at this point in his life.

Christianity and Power

I talk about John Lewis not simply because I want to tell you about a friend, but because I suspect there are many of us Christians in this generation who live with some of the same ambivalence about Christianity and success, Christianity and authority, Christianity and power. We live with the same kind of ambivalence that John Lewis does and we feel the tug and pull of it and wonder what to do about it. I believe that sort of ambivalence is peculiar to our generation. You may be sure our grandparents' generation did not experience it. No, this mood is new with us.

Fifty, eighty, or one hundred years ago the theme that Protestants and Catholics alike shared about the Christian future was essentially this: the church in the century ahead would become triumphant. The missionary movement was not basically a movement to bring agriculture or medicine or education to other countries. It was a movement to convert others to the Christian faith. When we sing the songs in our hymnal about the church triumphant, we may sing them metaphorically, but our grandparents sang them believing that it was the reality that was to come. The vision of the Christian church that our grandparents lived with was that the church, Christianity, would one day be the faith that the people of the planet shared. It would be the uniting, victorious religion.

That vision of Christianity has come under a most intense and a very appropriate criticism in our generation. For instance, as scholars and critics have examined it, they have discovered that it may be partly gospel, but it also is very much prejudice. That vision of the church triumphant has been wedded in the past to the colonial empires that the white races have pressed upon the races of color on this globe. It has been wedded to prejudicial visions that assume that men will forever be superior to women, that women should never rise to positions of authority or power. As we've criticized that vision that our grandparents held, we've decided that we have to cast out those prejudices. And the church to this day is in the process of fighting those prejudices that it has wrongly assumed were part of Christ's gospel. That fight against the prejudices must continue. Whites are not better than blacks, and men are not better than women; there is nothing in the gospel to justify such prejudicial assumptions.

The kind of ambivalence that John Lewis and other Christians in this generation of ours live with is partly generated by that very act of throwing out the prejudices. Luke 11:24-26 talks about driving out an evil spirit and leaving a vacuum at center, a vacuum that ultimately is filled by other evils that come in to replace the one that has been removed. I wonder if that vacuum is not precisely the danger and the cause of the kind of ambivalence that Christians live with today. The vacuum may bring about the kind of conflict we feel between what our Christian faith means and the possibilities of success that lie before us as individuals.

John Lewis is going through a crisis in faith and he's not the only one. It's something that can affect every one of us. That ambivalence that has come as we Christians have decided that we have to throw out the prejudices of the past has, I believe, allowed several false ideals of Christianity, what I call false commandments, to rise up and lay hold of us. The false ideals are neither healthy nor Christian, and yet I suspect that many Christians unwittingly live by these commandments as if they were gospel.

False Commandment One: Thou Shalt Not Hurt Anyone's Feelings

How often we make Christianity something that's no different from mere inoffensiveness! We act as though the last thing on earth we ought to do as Christians is to offer criticism to someone else. As a consequence we learn to keep the truth suppressed within us. Many of us live for years and years with jobs or in marriages or in family relationships in which we've decided simply not to tell the truth. If we tell it, we do so in such a shallow and superficial way that we never really get to the point or say anything about the deepest, most central hurts and joys that are in our lives because we might hurt someone else's feelings. We claim, of course, that we are following Christ in all this. The vision of Christ that we have when we say we're following him by being inoffensive is certainly not the Christ of the gospel. It's a sort of spiritual equivalent of Merv Griffin, a kind of mush-mouthed savior, who just keeps everyone happy and keeps the conversation rolling along.

The Christ of the gospel is clearly willing to say the truth that he sees even at the cost of anger or tears and ultimately at the cost of terrible retaliation to himself. Jesus is not just blandly critical of the Pharisees; he is vituperatively, explicitly critical of the Pharisees, calling them vipers, whitewashed tombs, blind guides. There is very little that is merely inoffensive about Jesus of Nazareth. Jesus is very much committed to speaking the truth, in love, to those who will listen to it and trusts that the truth, when spoken in love, can transform lives. A false commandment abroad in our age flies the banner of Christianity but ought not do it, and that commandment is "Thou shalt not hurt anyone else's feelings." Please understand, I do not urge you to go out and ride roughshod over those with whom you live or work. However, the equation that says that being Christian is being bland and inoffensive is false to the gospel and crippling to human living. There are false commandments that lay hold of us and keep us from following Christ. They can lead us to make exactly the wrong decision.

False Commandment Two: Thou Shalt Not Excel in Ways That Make Others Uneasy

The word from almost every corner is that the standards of quality that once marked American life and work are eroding. Mediocrity rather than excellence becomes the norm. The recent report of the President's Commission on Education is only one of many possible examples: Our schools are failing to educate. Similarly, our industries are failing to compete, and our leaders are failing to lead. What has happened is as much a spiritual as an economic or political phenomenon. It seems we simply don't care as much as we once did about doing whatever we do in the best possible fashion.

Robert M. Pirsig, in his fine book *Zen and the Art of Motorcycle Maintenance*, writes about this spiritual failure, this failure to care. He finds it pervasive in his experience, present not only

in his professional work (as a writer of computer manuals) but
also in his avocation (motorcycling):

> While at work I was thinking about this lack of care in the digital
> computer manuals I was editing . . . they were full of errors,
> ambiguities, omissions . . . you had to read them six times to make
> any sense out of them. But what struck me for the first time was
> the agreement of these manuals with the spectator attitude I had
> seen in the shop. These were spectator manuals. It was built into
> the format of them. Implicit in every line is the idea that, "Here
> is the machine, isolated in time and space from everything else in
> the universe. It has no relationship to you, you have no relationship
> to it, other than to turn certain switches, maintain voltage levels,
> check for error conditions . . . ' and so on. That's it. The mechanics
> in their attitude toward the machine (Pirsig's motorcycle) were
> really taking no different attitude from the manual's toward the
> machine or from the attitude I had when I brought it in there. We
> were all spectators. It then occurred to me, there is no manual that
> deals with the real business of motorcycle maintenance, the most
> important aspect of all. *Caring about what you're doing is considered*
> *either unimportant or taken for granted* [emphasis added].[1]

Why this flight from excellence? Why this lack of caring about
quality?

Certainly part of the answer is that for years we naively believed that America was the most sophisticated, quality producer
in the world, that since our wealth was unparalleled, our supremacy would go unchallenged. That smug mythology has
come under withering fire in recent years. In one market after
another—from automobiles to cameras, from videotapes to sil-
icon chips—overseas producers have presented winning products.

Another part of the answer lies in our very democratic heritage
and is the dark and difficult side of one of our highest and most
cherished beliefs: equality. We strive for it. We pass laws to
ensure it. All this is fine; yet in the process we can give the
message that to be excellent is somehow too showy, undemo-
cratic, gauche. The stories are endless of workers who could
produce more and would do so gladly, but they fear embar-
rassing those slower souls who work beside them. "Thou shalt
not excel in ways that make others uneasy."

William Manchester has written a marvelous book about Winston Churchill. It's the first of what he projects to be several
volumes on Churchill's life. It's called *The Last Lion* and the first
volume deals with Churchill's life up to the beginning of World

War II. Winston Churchill as a politician, as an orator, as a writer, as a journalist towered above people of his generation. He was committed unequivocally to excellence and, of course, he made many enemies. The remarkable thing about Winston Churchill, and the remarkable thing about the age in which he lived, was that even his enemies believed in the excellence he showed in debates, in writing, in politics.

One of the themes that Manchester strikes in his book is that on those occasions when Winston Churchill lost elections to Parliament, he regularly heard by letter from political opponents in Parliament who told him that *they hoped he would win next time*. Why did they want him to win? Not because they agreed with him; they didn't agree with him. Not because they loved him; they did not love him a bit. They say that he brought to parliamentary debate a standard of excellence without which the nation could not aspire to the excellence they wanted the nation to attain. Manchester, after he talks about excellence, goes on to say that such excellence is no longer possible in the democracies today, because we have supplanted the impulse to excellence with an impulse toward equality, a sense of leveling, of making sure that no one is too much better than anyone else.

Little by little "Thou shalt not excel in ways that make others uneasy" has crept into Christianity. Have you felt the pressure of that false commandment in your life? I believe that many of us who are Christians feel it.

Ask if that's true to the gospel. What did Christ do when he called disciples? Did he call Peter and John, these fishermen, and say to them, "Come with me and I will make you a 10 percent better fisherman than you are today"? Not for a moment. Christ called them to be excellent. He transformed them. He called them to be fishers of men. Did he go to Matthew, a tax collector, and say, "I could increase your income by 15 percent if you follow my principles"? Not at all. The beginning of the Christian movement did not come out of an impulse to make everyone a little bit better. It came out of Christ's calling individual men and women, transforming their lives, and trusting that changing them would change the world.

Christianity is a call to excellence for the individual, for you and for me. False commandments lay hold of us because of the ambivalence we live with, because in casting out the old prejudices we've allowed a vacuum to form wherein these false thoughts of our day can lay hold of the gospel in inappropriate ways.

False Commandment Three: Thou Shalt Keep Thy Deepest Beliefs to Thyself

Oh yes, I know there are many Christians who don't live by that, and we at the liberal end of Christianity are often uneasy with those Christians. There are fundamentalist Christians, evangelical Christians who will gladly collar you and tell you more than you would like to know about Jesus Christ, and I am not saying that we ought to imitate that. I don't think there's any room for loudmouthed, oppressive coercion in Christianity, but I fear that we in the liberal churches in particular have gone too far in being very soft-spoken about what we believe. We simply do not share it.

I remember a marvelous conversation I had with Rabbi Stan Davids, a colleague and friend who shared several dialogue sermons with me. The difficulty with dialogue sermons (which involve two people sharing a dialogue in place of one person preaching a sermon in worship) is that they become bland and disinteresting—a recitation of points of agreement rather than a real exchange of beliefs. Stan wanted to avoid this problem, so when we sat down to plan those talks, he insisted that what was needed was not bland agreement between us, but a willingness to honestly and lovingly argue. We needed not to hedge for a moment on the areas about which we disagreed: Jews and Christians. I believe that's the way Christians can communicate with those of another faith: not by denying what we believe but by being crystal clear about our belief and how deeply we hold it and at the same time offering love and respect to those who differ from us. However, there is a commandment abroad that says, "Thou shalt keep thy deepest beliefs to thyself." Particularly in the workplace, particularly in the commerce of daily life, don't bring them up, please.

Psychologist Vladimir DeLissovoy, talking about the triumph of the psychological method in our world, says that we have adopted a stance that he calls "dogmatic neutrality." Dogmatic neutrality insists that all ideas are equal and anyone who wants to take a position relative to ideas or values must be dogmatically neutral—not just neutral but dogmatically neutral. He must insist that all ideas are equal. How many times have you heard in a discussion group, even in church, "Now there are no right or wrong answers. We are only expressing opinions here"? Don't misunderstand. I think that statement is often the right way to begin a discussion; but I believe, too, that when we Christians hear it, there is something in our souls that says, "Yes there is a right answer!" We may not have private, exclusive claim to what that right answer is, but we are certainly seekers after what that truth is. We believe contrary to those who insist on dogmatic neutrality. We believe that there is out there, perhaps beyond our comprehension, some right answer to which we can aspire.

"Thou shalt keep thy deepest beliefs to thyself." Have you felt the weight of this false commandment on your heart and soul when you wished to say that you deeply believed but knew that it would be against the code?

False Commandment Four: Thou Shalt Be Concerned for Means but Not for Ends

Care for process but not for outcomes. Let me say immediately that that is, in part, a very necessary and important conclusion for this generation of ours—to be very concerned for means. We have lived through a terrible period in history, and to a large extent we still live in such a period: Ends, or outcomes, have been used to justify all sorts of atrocities. We have lived through the eras of Hitler and Stalin. We live today on a globe in which vast totalitarian police states feel completely free to resist the expression of human freedom in the name of some grand scheme of human equality down the road. Yes, we need to be deeply concerned about the means by which we make decisions, by which we govern ourselves and make our choices. We need to be sure that those means are just.

We must also be concerned that the means are effective. Ends do count; there are outcomes; jobs must get done. Sometimes in our fascination with the appropriate process we stand in danger of forgetting this.

Thomas J. Peters and Robert H. Waterman, Jr., in their remarkable book *In Search of Excellence* present their findings of their recent studies of seventy-five excellent American corporations. Almost without exception they found that the excellent corporations were able to cut through the potentially paralyzing focus on process and move toward results. The example they give of Dana Corporation is typical. Dana is today a three-billion-dollar corporation making unexotic, "low-tech" devices such as brass propeller blades and gearboxes and supplying the automotive and truck-building industry. For years Dana floated along at the industry average in productivity. Then a whirlwind in the person of Rene McPherson was appointed chief executive officer, and the company's productivity and profits took off. In simple terms, what McPherson did was to shift the company's attention toward caring for its people and helping them get results. He cut through the process-oriented bureaucracy and opened communications. One of his first acts was to throw out the twenty-two inches of policy manuals he inherited. He replaced them with a one-page statement of philosophy focusing on "productive people." He began to let the managers and employees of each of Dana's seventy-five plants have almost complete say about how the job got done as long as it got done. In short, he trusted people more than formal procedures and got remarkable results.[2]

A false commandment that threatens to paralyze our life and work these days is: "Thou shalt be concerned for means but not for ends." In following that misguided commandment we can make process our god and blind ourselves to the realities and needs before us.

I was at a denominational meeting not long ago in Cleveland, and one of the things that I heard from a denominational executive illustrates this problem of fascination with means to the exclusion of ends. The subject under debate was the appointment of an individual to a particular post of major responsibility in the denomination. The questions that were being raised had to do with whether this individual was equal to the task, whether this person was the best, even adequate, for the job. One of the executives responded that what was important to him was that all the correct processes had been followed: the right committees had met and voted and the right documents had been filed. Hence, once the processes had been appropriately followed, it really didn't matter what the outcome was—it had to be correct.

We have lived with this notion for so long in this generation of ours that we've become deeply concerned for due process but not as concerned for justice. We have lived with it for so long that in areas of education we have become tremendously concerned about whether or not the appropriate educational theories and policies are followed and the right courses are taken, but not adequately concerned about whether or not anything is learned. This notion has been around for so long that in areas of work and productivity we've become deeply concerned that the proper sort of negotiations are followed, the right documents are filed, and the correct legal procedures happen but not with whether or not the product works. In short we've become fascinated with the concern for rights, to some extent excluding an appropriate concern for the responsibilities of our citizens.

There is a commandment abroad, one that is not in keeping with the gospel, that tells us that we have to be forever concerned with processes almost to the exclusion of worrying about what the outcomes are.

Facing the New Enemy of Ambivalence

We live in a time of ambivalence. Not only my friend John Lewis but all of us can feel the tug, the pull within our hearts as we try to find what it means to live by the gospel in this age. We have appropriately begun the task of clearing the house we live in of the evil spirit of prejudices that have blighted it too long; prejudice against people of color, prejudice against women, prejudice against minorities. In the process, however, we have endangered ourselves by allowing false commandments to lay hold of us. The fact is that as Christians we are not called always to be sweet, innocuous, or inoffensive. We are called always to speak the truth in love. As Christians we are not called to hold our abilities in check and cast aside every high ambition and every striving for excellence that is possible for us because our excellence might make someone else uneasy. Rather, God calls us to aspire to the best, the highest talents we can master. As Christians we are not called to censor our beliefs and never share them with others. We are called to offer to others that mighty truth that has claimed us and to offer it with humility and respect for different beliefs. As Christians we are not called to be so concerned with means and processes that we are indifferent to results. We are called to be sure that both means and ends serve God's purpose.

There are false commandments carrying the gospel's banner today. We in the Christian community, while ridding ourselves of the prejudices of the past, need to be sure that we do not fill our hearts with the prejudices of the present.

11

Captivity's Attraction—(Or, Is It Time to Grow Up?)

And the LORD said to Moses, "Gather for me seventy men of the elders of Israel, whom you know to be the elders of the people and officers over them; and bring them to the tent of meeting, and let them take their stand there with you. And I will come down and talk with you there; and I will take some of the spirit which is upon you and put it upon them; and they shall bear the burden of the people with you, that you may not bear it yourself alone. And say to the people, 'Consecrate yourselves for tomorrow, and you shall eat meat; for you have wept in the hearing of the LORD, saying, "Who will give us meat to eat? For it was well with us in Egypt." Therefore the Lord will give you meat, and you shall eat'" (Numbers 11:16-18).

A few years ago Shana Alexander wrote a book about Patty Hearst entitled *Anyone's Daughter*. Do you remember Patty Hearst? She is the heiress of the famous Hearst family, owners of a publishing empire, who was kidnapped, held captive, and ultimately became a member of the Symbionese Liberation Army (SLA) group that had abducted her. Miss Alexander was interested in how this astonishing transformation had come about in Patty Hearst.

Patty had been raised in a particular tradition of respect for law, order, property, and propriety. Her family had been anything but radical. While Patty was certainly a child of the sixties and subject to all that went with that era, she had shown no sympathy for or interest in the various self-styled liberation armies of that time. Yet, something happened to Patty Hearst. Under the influence of Cinque, the SLA commander, and his colleagues, she underwent a dramatic change. She did not remain a victim and a captive but became a willing participant in the work of this small band of terrorists. She was, in a few weeks, transformed from the staid, proper heiress into a rifle-carrying, slogan-shouting, soldier in the urban underground. Remember that amazing videotape of the bank robbery that showed Patty Hearst holding a rifle, aiming it not at the members of the Symbionese Liberation Army but at the people that were being robbed? She had become a radical, a terrorist. She had been changed.

Shana Alexander's book talks about how that conversion happened and why, and she makes the point that it could have happened to anyone in similar circumstances. That was an outrageous claim at the time, for people were trying to explain Patty's change in a variety of ways. Some thought that she'd had some falling out with her parents. Others said she'd been radicalized on a college campus and maybe the kidnapping was merely a sham with which she had fully gone along. People felt that there must be some easy explanation. What Miss Alexander showed is that there is within every one of us a certain attraction toward captivity. We all have a desire, if you will, to identify with our captors when we find ourselves in such a situation or if we should find ourselves in such a situation.

Miss Alexander quotes a number of studies by psychologists and others that demonstrate that people who are held hostage in airplane hijackings and prison takeovers rather quickly learn to identify completely with their captors. Captives learn to watch them, to come to know them, to sympathize with them, and to do willingly what their captors ask. That's what happened to Patty Hearst. She discovered not just in her mind but in her very life that there was a certain attraction to captivity. You see, in captivity life becomes dramatically simplified. There is now only one person to please. Before, when she was living on her own with a whole range of choices before her, life may have been confusing and threatening. When she became a hostage, it became clear that there was only one direction for her; only one individual, Cinque, needed to be watched and known and followed. A certain purity of purpose emerged from giving herself to this new movement, from giving in to captivity.

It's an old story that's been told before. Hanna Arendt in her book *Eichmann in Jerusalem*, talks about Adolf Eichmann, who engineered the mass slaughter of Jews in Europe, and about how he took control of Jewish communities one by one across Europe. Control came, of course, with troops and guns but also in a more subtle way. He would come into a town with a small band of people who were loyal to him. His first act would be to call an assembly of the Judenrat, the council of Jewish elders who were the decision makers in the Jewish community. He'd sit down with them calmly, kind and sensitive in his demeanor, and explain that a certain number of people needed to be sent to work camps from their community. He would be glad, if they wished, to make the decisions himself about who would get on the trains and go off to the concentration camps. Eichmann felt, however, that it would be better if they, the leaders, made the decision about who went. Time after time those Jewish elders decided that, yes, it would be better if they made the decision. So one Jewish community after another all across Europe was emptied out, all in a most efficient manner with very few German troops involved because this cunning, evil man, convinced his captives to cooperate. Captivity is attractive. Even though the Jewish elders knew they were faced with certain doom, there seemed a way to maintain at least a semblance of control when they were able to make decisions about who should go and who should stay.

There is an attraction about captivity. There is a certain covered-up eagerness in us to give our lives into the control of others because it simplifies things and makes life seem purposeful and clear. Captivity's story is very old. Older than Patty Hearst. Older than the death of six million Jews in Europe.

The passage from the book of Numbers which begins this chapter is about Israel in the wilderness on its way to freedom. The people had come out of Egypt where they had been slaves, and now they were kind of in between, no longer slaves and not yet landowners in the new Promised Land. Not yet free but no longer captive, they were just out there in the wilderness. It was exciting. It was also frightening, and after some years it came to be more than a little boring as well. The specific complaint in this case was about food.

God and Moses thought they had solved the problem of food. The solution was manna. You remember manna from your Sunday church school lessons. Manna was the solution. The problem was that people gradually got tired of it. What was manna?

Well, scholars have looked into this and they aren't very clear; at least they are equivocal about what it was. The Scriptures say it was similar to coriander seed (Exodus 16:31). Does that help you? It doesn't help me. What was manna? Well, I like to think of it as a biblical version of Special K, if you will. It had all the vitamins and minerals and all the minimum daily requirements in it. The problem was that in taste tests it kept losing out to Cocoa Puffs and Sugar Pops and things like that.

What was manna? Well, any college student could tell us that manna is like dorm food or dining hall meals. If you've ever eaten in a dorm or a dining hall, you know that night after night you go there and you see things that look a little different. Perhaps tonight the food has been fried instead of boiled. Still, in your own heart you know that fundamentally, chemically, there is no difference between tonight's meal and last night's meal. Manna was like that. It got on people's nerves just as dorm food gets on students' nerves. You could conjure up a scene if you'd like. A little boy, say a nine- or ten-year-old, has been playing in the Israelite camp. He comes home hungry.

"Mom, what's for dinner?"

"Mannaburgers, Davey."

"Mannaburgers again!" says Davey.

Manna was getting boring. In the midst of this story about boredom and somewhere between freedom and captivity is lodged one of those great, magnificent, hidden phrases of the Bible. It's not a well-known one, or a memory verse, but it ought to be. It's the kind of thing you ought to write on an index card and put on your desk or on your refrigerator. The phrase, spoken by the people in the midst of all their complaining about the food, is this: "It was well with us in Egypt."

The children of Israel were now far enough from Egypt and its terror that they remembered it with longing and affection. They forgot, or chose not to remember, the brutal realities—that they were slaves; that they had harsh, murderous taskmasters; that their children were taken from them. The terrible realities were forgotten. What was remembered was that the food was better. Perhaps there wasn't enough of it every night, but at least it was different. It wasn't manna. "It was well with us in Egypt."

What Holds Us?

There is a certain attraction to captivity, and it's true not only for those Israelites in the wilderness but also for us. What is it, for example, that holds us captive, that is attractive to us and lays claim to us, to you and me? What is it that keeps us from coming to our full strength in life, from really growing up?

One of the great joys and privileges of being a pastor is the opportunity to talk in depth and in detail with all kinds of people. It's very special to hear from young and old alike, to have friends share their deepest hopes and darkest fears. One of the themes that comes through from people of all ages is this: "Somehow, I never completely grew up." There's probably not a person I know who couldn't in one way or another say that about themselves. No matter how gray our hair is, how old we are, or how young we are, there is some part of us that knows we haven't fully matured. You can see it in many ways.

For example, a number of us are parents, and I am sure to our children we look extremely mature, self-confident, and certain. But think about the decisions that we make about those kids. How much certainty do we really have and how much worry do we have in the midst of deciding whether our children should go to this school or that school? Should our children study a musical instrument or spend the time doing something else? To our kids we look mature and self-confident, but inside ourselves there is a good deal more uncertainty than we let on. Somehow we haven't yet, we know, come to that full maturity. I know people who are grandparents, some who are patriarchs and matriarchs within their families. People look up to them. Their families love them and respect them. Yet, if you could look inside the secret heart and mind of those very individuals, you would also find some considerable elements of uncertainty, doubt, worry. It's part of the human condition. We don't finally reach that point where we can say: "Now, there, I've done it. I'm complete, I'm fully grown up." All of us have a sense that we could do better than we have.

Something, though, holds us back; something lays claim to us, a kind of Egypt or captivity to which we give ourselves and which keeps us childlike and immature. Maybe we decide to turn our life decisions over to the corporation we work for; maybe we decide that we'll let some family member dictate how

things should go. Maybe we decide that the church should tell
us how to run things. Maybe we join some fraternal organization
or any of a number of clubs and let them dominate our decisions
and control our time. There's always a temptation to turn our
freedom over to someone else and live in a kind of attractive
captivity that simplifies life.

Paul says that we are called beyond that kind of captivity. Just
like the Israelites in the desert, we're to be on our way toward
a greater freedom and a greater maturity. He says: "When I was
a child, I spoke like a child, I thought like a child, I reasoned
like a child; when I became a man, I gave up childish ways" (1
Corinthians 13:11). "I gave up childish ways"; that is an agenda
item for most of us. How do you do it, whether you are a
teenager or a grandparent? How do you begin to give up childish
ways that have held you back from growing up, from coming
to full maturity?

Marks of Responsible Adulthood

Psychiatrist Erik Erikson has made a career of studying ado-
lescence. He says that there are three tasks that are *absolutely
necessary* and *must* be completed if youth is to be completed, if
one is to move into responsible adulthood: an identity tied to
some competence; sexuality bound to a style of intimacy; and
the anticipation of becoming, before long, responsible for the
next generation.[1] It's interesting to hear a great psychiatrist
confirm some of the basic truths that all great ethical systems
teach. What is required of us if we're to complete our youth is
competence, intimacy, and responsibility. We can't make it into
maturity without them. We know that and yet we so easily lose
hold of those truths in the midst of life's demands.

An Identity Tied to Competence

There's a certain rhetoric abroad today that says: "You're not
really what you do. Don't identify yourself with your profession
and the things you can achieve and the things you can make.
You're not just what you do, you're what you are. There's some
essence of you that is more than just your job."

That's true, of course (indeed, I've agreed with the idea and
even advocated it in chapter 6), and yet one can push that too
far. Erikson's claim, and it's something all of us know at a very

fundamental level, is that unless we've learned to master some things, to become not only competent but also excellent in some areas of life, we'll never reach the kind of maturity that's required of us. We'll never step beyond childishness and youthfulness. We'll always be somebody's little boy or little girl or lackey.

Every September we church people see young men and women who have grown up in our midst go off to college. It is a time of decision making and commitment, a time for those young persons to say: "I am going to become as good as I can be in this area of study." We need to say to those young people: "We're with you. We know it won't come easily, but we believe that it's extremely important for you to master some things, some skills, not to be the best at everything on earth, but to be the best you can be in the area that you choose for yourself. Insofar as we are capable, we'll stand behind you in this time of decision because it's one of the necessary steps to maturity."

As a church we ought to say that as well to all the rest of us; the need to achieve competence in some area of life is not something that is finished when college is over or when high school ends or when we learn a trade. It continually rises up before us. One problem comes and is solved and another problem comes. The kind of competence that's required of us is lifelong.

Intimacy

Erikson's second requirement for reaching maturity is a sexuality bound to a style of intimacy. That's a word that needs very much to be heard in this generation. Turn on the TV during any evening and you'll see endless accounts of sexuality completely divorced from intimacy. The private eye manages to charm the girl and by the time the show ends they're in bed together or on the way there. By next week the girl has disappeared into some other serial or sitcom; so our hero charms a new girl. There's no intimacy at all—just one casual sexual encounter after another, so much so that it starts to become a pattern that people think is healthy and wise and enjoyable. Ultimately, however, it's destructive and will enforce a certain childishness on people, keeping them from coming to maturity. Erikson's point is that when real sexuality comes into full maturity, it is bound to intimacy, it is shared with someone we love in a way that we would not love any other soul on earth.

We live in an age when marriages fail one after the other. In some cities as many as 60 percent of the marriages end in divorce. Now, to be sure, divorce is necessary sometimes, and it ought not carry the kind of moral stigma that it did a generation ago. At the same time a word needs to be said for perseverance in marriage. There's a marvelous scene in Alan Alda's movie *The Four Seasons*. The movie is about three couples that have been friends for years and have always vacationed together. After they vacation together for about twenty consecutive summers, one of the couples gets a divorce. The husband remarries and brings his new wife on the vacation on the twenty-first year. This causes all sorts of fret, fear, and uproar, which culminates in Carol Burnett (who plays Alda's wife) confronting the re-married husband, telling him how disgusted she is with him for his divorce, and saying, "Why didn't you just stay in there and fight it out like the rest of us?"

A word needs to be said for staying in there and fighting it out like the rest of us. The promises we have are not that marriage is always smooth and easy. Intimacy is not an easy thing, but it does give us the best opportunity we have for permanence. It gives us the chance to grow up into the full meaning of those words spoken in marriage, "As long as we both shall live." Today, however, there is the temptation to give in to that kind of easy sexuality that's divorced from intimacy.

The following was a letter to Dear Abby:

> I am a twenty-three-year-old liberated woman who has been on the pill for two years. It's getting pretty expensive and I think my boyfriend should share half the cost, but I don't know him well enough to discuss money with him.[2]

Yes, the letter is for real. That's sexuality divorced from inti-macy. There is no coming to maturity, no freedom from captiv-ity's attraction in such a relationship.

Responsibility

The third requirement Erikson lists for moving to a completion of our youth and into maturity is to take responsibility for the future generation. Taking responsibility for the future generation can take many forms. For some it will be the simple but arduous task of raising children to adulthood. For others it may be the nurturing of our vital institutions—businesses, churches, schools, hospitals—keeping them strong and thriving not merely for our own gain, but for those who will need them after we are gone.

For Wendell Berry taking responsibility involves farming. Wendell Berry is a fascinating man, an intellectual, a guiding spirit of the environmental movement. He's a professor of English, a novelist, a poet, an essayist. In short he has gained the world's esteem. What has gained his esteem is not merely the life of literature and the mind but the life of the earth and of the soil. Wendell Berry is first and foremost a farmer. He lives and farms with his family in Port Royal, Kentucky. He farms organically. He's chosen this way of farming not out of faddishness or love of novelty, but because he has seen the ruin that heavy, mechanized, chemically dependent farming methods have made of the land on which he lives. Much of the damage to the land came during the lifetime of his parents, grandparents, and great-grandparents who worked the same property that Berry now works. Steep hillsides were plowed, and years of erosion have left them rocky and infertile. Once-rich soil has been over-farmed and worn out. The buildup of chemicals in the soil, chemicals from commercial fertilizers, has destroyed the very life of the soil itself.

All this has happened in the name of productivity and progress; largely it has been done by people who farmed the land until it was worn out and then moved on to new land. Wendell Berry has chosen to stay on the land and spend his life returning it to health. Why? Because there is only one earth, and land once destroyed takes generations to rebuild. Why? Because the generations yet to come will need the land, the soil, the earth—rich and healthy.

In one of his novels, Wendell Berry creates a character, Matt Feltner, who really speaks for Berry. The time is World War II. Matt's son Virgil, who was to take over the farm when Matt retired, is missing in action. Matt is fifty years old; his future and the land's future seem very uncertain. Will Virgil be found? Will anyone farm the land? In the midst of these questions, Matt still goes out to clear and renew the overgrown, neglected fields of his sick cousin Roger Merchant. Berry writes: "But a few days ago (before the news that Virgil is missing had come), if he had considered expending time and bother on this land, he would have considered also the possibility that he might be able to buy it. But now Virgil is missing, and Matt needs no more land for himself. He is too old now to need it—if he ever did. This new work must be done for the sake of the land itself—and for the sake of no one he can foresee, someone who will come later, who will depend then on what is done now."[3]

Where is God calling you to come to maturity by taking responsibility for the future generation or generations, to take responsibility for people you may neither know nor foresee but "who will depend then, on what is done now"?

Captivity has a certain attraction. It's easier than growing up, and yet we're called to maturity. That's what Paul talks about; that's what Erik Erikson talks about when he says that what's required of us is competence, intimacy, and responsibility. To those things we Christians can add one more mark of maturity and freedom. Paul says, "When I became a man I gave up childish ways," but paradoxically Christ says, "Whoever does not receive the kingdom of God like a child shall not enter it" (Luke 18:17).

In addition to competence, intimacy, and responsibility Christians rely on trust, trust in a God who does not finally forsake us. We believe that in every frightening new situation there is One whom we can trust, One to whom we can turn and rely on. Those people in the desert, tired of eating manna, decided it had been well with them in Egypt. There is always the hazard of deciding in favor of captivity when we are faced with freedom. The choice we're called to is of the future, not of the past. There is where it will be well with us with God.

12

Life Without Pretense

And a ruler asked him, "Good Teacher, what shall I do to inherit eternal life?" And Jesus said to him, "Why do you call me good? No one is good but God alone. You know the commandments: 'Do not commit adultery, Do not kill, Do not steal, Do not bear false witness, Honor your father and mother.'" And he said, "All these I have observed from my youth." And when Jesus heard it, he said to him, "One thing you still lack. Sell all that you have and distribute to the poor, and you will have treasure in heaven; and come, follow me." But when he heard this he became sad, for he was very rich (Luke 18:18-23).

Perhaps the hardest aspect of decision making is facing the realities in front of us at decision time. Earlier in this book I touched upon the danger of living with pretense, that is, living in a dream world that we wish existed instead of living in the real world God created. Here, in the final chapter, I want to explore that danger in detail and offer a Christian response to it.

You've probably heard of Norman Cousins. He first came into the public eye through journalism. For many years he was the widely respected editor and publisher of *The Saturday Review*. In more recent years, Cousins has become well known for his interest in the treatment and cure of disease through holistic medicine. His book *Anatomy of an Illness* detailed his own long, successful battle with a life-threatening collagen disorder. The book advocates, among other approaches to treatment, the use of joy, love, and laughter to restore health. In his most recent book, *The Healing Heart*, Cousins tells about yet another serious affliction that he has dealt with successfully. Once again he used a combination of the best medical advice available and the positive experience of faith and love and high good humor, this time to bring about his recovery from a serious heart attack.

In the course of his recovery, after it became clear that he would, in fact, regain strength and be able to return to full activity, Cousins's wife and daughter decided to hold a surprise party for him on the first anniversary of his heart attack. Cousins learned of this and decided on a surprise of his own. He contacted a neighbor and friend, Dev Freedman, head of the Make-up Department at Universal Studios in California. Dev and his wife had been invited to the surprise party, and Cousins enlisted their aid in pulling off his own prank. He arranged to be completely made up at Universal and to attend his own surprise party disguised so that no one would be able to recognize him.

When the appointed day came, Norman Cousins presented himself at the studio where in an hour's time he was given a rust-colored beard, a wig, and a cosmetic application on his face that changed the shape of his nose, eyes, and mouth. When he looked in the mirror at the end of the session, he could not recognize himself. He drove to the Freedman's house, rang the bell, and laughed uproariously at their bewildered response. They, too, had not recognized him.

The next stop was the party, which took place at his own home. He arrived with the Freedmans and was introduced as their friend, Dr. Morton, from England. Cousins made the most of his opportunity. He explained that he had heard that Californians are exceptionally open and friendly, whereupon he proceeded around the room kissing, patting, and pinching all the women—none of whom recognized him, though they were all close friends. Dr. Morton quickly became the object of much whispering and many censorious glances.

After a half hour or so with guests growing weary with the peculiar Dr. Morton and anxious that Cousins had not shown up yet, Cousins decided it was time to bring the masquerade to an end—something which could be awkward, except that, typically, he was prepared for it. He walked to the organ that occupied one corner of the living room, seated himself, and started to play one of his signature pieces. As soon as the music started, Cousins's daughter Candis, at the time making party preparations in the kitchen, ran into the living room, crying, "Daddy's home." The guests gathered at the piano bench, the makeup came off, and there was laughter and welcoming all around.

In Cousins's case, the disguise was a great hit. It served its purpose when it was on—no one recognized the guest of honor. Too, it served its purpose when it came off; it gave everyone a great jolt of surprise and laughter.

Disguises

When put together well, disguises of costumes and concealing makeup can be marvelous in their place. Now, what about the other possibility—the demonic, crippling possibility—that also comes with the disguises we choose and wear in life? What if the disguise never comes off? What if in our awkwardness and fear we choose continuously to live shielded and unrevealed, existing as an unwelcome, unrecognized guest even at our own party? This deadly condition is neither as strange nor as uncommon as it may at first sound.

Howard Campbell, Jr., the main character in Kurt Vonnegut's book *Mother Night,* is a patriotic American citizen, who during World War II accepts his government's dangerous undercover assignment. By becoming a deeply placed and reliable spy, he is to penetrate the Nazi high command and help stop the terrible onslaught of Hitler's armies. Campbell, dedicated, brave, and single-minded, pursues his assignment with great devotion and skill. His work takes years and requires his constant and close association with Nazi leaders. It forces him to write a lot of slanderous, even murderous propaganda against the Allies. The consequence of it all is that at the end of the war, when the Nazis are defeated, Howard Campbell, Jr., feels defeated, too. He experiences no victory, only lostness. So completely had he masqueraded that he could not give up the pretense, the act, once the need for it was over. Vonnegut says of this story: "This is the only story of mine whose moral I know. I don't think it's a marvelous moral; I simply happen to know what it is: We are what we pretend to be, so we must be very careful about what we pretend to be."[1]

We are what we pretend to be. One of the great dangers in life is that we become at ease with pretense. Somewhere along the way we put on a disguise that seems beautiful and useful at the time, but it later proves limiting and crippling. However, we grow accustomed to it, so much so that we literally grow into it—as Chinese women of a century ago found that their feet grew into the painful shape into which they were bound in childhood. Does this come close to home for you? Have you found yourself living a pretense for too long, disguised as one thing when really you're another? Have you found it difficult to peel off beard and mask and wig because they have grown to be part of your very flesh and person—so much so that you wonder what, in fact, you'd be without this disguise? Good decisions require taking off our disguises.

It's discomfiting to discover or admit about ourselves that we are what we pretend to be—or at least are at risk of becoming only what we pretend to be. It's hard to face in ourselves, but far easier to see and name in others. All of us have friends and acquaintances to whom we've seen this happen. They've become what their clothes or role or office or position say they are. I can't tell you how many clergy friends I have who, somewhere in the years between seminary and today, have stopped being persons and become only clergy. It's fascinating and troubling, for I knew them when they were flesh-and-blood individuals with different hopes, rough edges, personal quirks and foibles, real joy and real sadness, and real anger. Now, in many cases it's all gone—washed away in some great bath we in this profession too easily take. Now when a person asks what they believe or think or feel—"they" do not really answer at all—ministers answer. For that is what they know: what ministers think, what ministers feel, what ministers say in this or that situation.

This plague of pretense is, of course, not limited to clergy. (I name ministers only because I am a minister and am able to examine the profession up close.) We are all easily polluted by it as the years pass. Surely we've seen this phenomenon in many persons and many careers: doctors who can talk only like doctors; teachers who think only what teachers are supposed to think; truck drivers who have become nothing more nor less than truck drivers; homemakers who do nothing but make homes fit for the habitation of families.

A Test

If you would like to check yourself to see how much or how little pretense and masquerade you live with, try the following. You don't need pencil or paper. The test can be taken in the privacy of your own brain and heart. The phrase to check for in your thinking is *"I dare not."* Think of what follows as a sentence completion test. Search for a recurring sentence or thought that is loudly trumpeted in the silence of your brain but which is quite likely never spoken for others to hear.

I DARE NOT talk with my husband or wife about the real and deep fears I have about our marriage—naming the fears would give them power. (In truth, however, it is the very secrecy and silence which gives them power.)

I DARE NOT talk with the boss about problems at work. He has to think that I love what I'm doing and that nothing is wrong.

I DARE NOT say to my son how concerned, even worried, I am for him. He couldn't handle it. He'd only grow further away from me.

I DARE NOT even think of changing careers. I've invested so much in this one, and with the kids starting college next year I've got to stay where I am.

I DARE NOT tell my pastor, doctor, or best friend the inward doubts I live with. They'll think so much less of me.

Do you hear that phrase, too often, echoing inside the confines of your thoughts: *I dare not*? It is a flag, an indicator of accumulated pretense, of a dangerous buildup of sham. If left unattended and unaddressed, *I dare not* will drive out the real person God made you to be. It will take over the deep places of life by reducing everything you do to the perpetuation of a smiling fiction. One cannot forever live as a full, growing Christian human being with that constant *I dare not* controlling life and its most vital choices.

The real problem in living by pretense is that sooner or later we develop two separate lives: an inner life of true feeling, thought, and desire and an outer life of conformity, normality, and respectability. The longer we live with the two separate lives, the sadder, weaker, and unhappier we become. If we stay in that situation long enough, we risk ultimately killing the inner life altogether. We can choke it into silence and settle for living only at the surface, mistaking daily superficiality for all there is to life.

The Christian call is to put the inner and the outer together, to bring them into harmony with one another, to live without pretense. I don't mean to say that this is easy or that it is something that we can do once and for all and never have to worry about again. The continuing struggle for any Christian is to bring the inner truths and the outer actions into straight and healthy relationship with one another—to put off pretense, to end the masquerade. (I'll talk more about this in a moment when I look at the gospel story of the rich young ruler, a man who could not put the inner and the outer together.)

Two Traps

We who live in this generation are faced with two serious traps, or seductions, as we make the effort to answer God's call to end pretense and to make life whole. Both traps offer the false hope of removing us from the struggle to bring inner life and outer action together. Both offer the false promise that we can rise above and beyond that tension. The two phony escapes are *Escape via Isolation* and *Escape via Organization*. I think most of us are familiar with both traps although we may not call them by these names.

Escape via Isolation

Escape via Isolation promises that one day, if you make the right moves, you can remove yourself from any concern for the rest of humanity or from what other people think. You can, according to this seductive trap, build a life for you and you alone—where the inner and real you can be in complete control. J. M. Coetzee, a brilliant South African writer, in his book *The Life and Times of Michael K.*, has his hero, Michael K., seek exactly such a solution to his own life's problem. Michael K. is a young retarded black man living in the midst of civil war in South Africa. He is a peaceful, lonely soul. All his kin are dead. He cannot understand the armed rage and terror which swirls around him, so he seeks to escape it all by finding a place of isolated safety in the countryside. He flees from the besieged city of Cape Town and makes his way toward his mother's homeland.

Frightened and confused by the contrast between an outer civil war and his inner peaceful nature, he decides to climb higher and higher into the uninhabited central mountains. Finally, near the summit he finds a cave; he cuts brush for a bed on the cave floor, lies down, and thinks: " . . . surely no one will be mad enough to cross these plains, climb these mountains, search these rocks to find me; surely now that in all the world only I know where I am, I can think of myself as lost."[2]

"I can think of myself as lost." That is the great seduction of isolating ourselves. We believe, hope, or fantasize that we can remove ourselves from the belligerent demands of outer life. We can live isolated and lost—a rule unto ourselves, our inner world our only world. Unfortunately, Michael K. discovers that his escape and satisfaction are only temporary. Hunger and disease ultimately drive him from his isolated cave back into the warring company of human beings.

Has isolation tempted you? Its seductive call takes many forms: a cabin in the north woods; an island in the Pacific; running away to a new life in a new town; withdrawal into drugs or alcohol or some private, unassailable ideology. It will not finally work. God did not make us to live in isolation. And God did not call us to private, secret peace but to the struggle for honesty and wholeness, a struggle that must be played out in the company of others and in the face of the dangerous world.

Escape via Organization

The other great temptation in our day is Escape via Organization, that is, to remove ourselves from the struggle between inward beliefs and outward actions by plunging body and soul into a company, a university, a church—any organization that promises to give power and meaning to life, to answer all questions and doubts, and to make us whole. However, no organization, no matter how well run or committed it is, can effect these things.

John Kenneth Galbraith, writing about what he calls "Corporate Man," claims that almost all of us have to a great extent given our lives, our homes, and ourselves into the control of some large organization. In particular, those of us who rise to the top in such organizations (remember, I'm including churches, too; I'm not just throwing stones at others here) regularly do so at considerable, even enormous sacrifices of "the right to personal thought and expression." We reap large rewards but sometimes at "the expense of family, friends, sex, recreation, and sometimes health and effective control of alcoholic intake."[3]

We solve the enigma and struggle between outer and inner life by becoming the organization we're part of. We wind up with practically no separate life or identity apart from that organization. You can see the truth of Galbraith's claim simply by examining the experiences of corporate executives when they are out of work. Their reaction is often not merely that they've lost a job, but that they've lost themselves, literally not knowing who they are without the organization to offer nurture, identity, and influence.

Two great seductions, or traps, stand in the path of any twentieth-century man or woman seeking to answer Christ's call to authenticity and wholeness, to a healthy union of inner musts and outer realities. One is the trap of isolation, the fantasy that we do not need others and can live entirely by our inner light. The other is the trap of organization, the mistaken belief that with luck and hard work we can reach such a position of power that our inner wants and outer actions are potent enough to be the same, in other words that we and the organization can become one.

The Price of Pretense

Christ's call is to a life without pretense, a life in which the inner world of thoughts and desires is connected to the outer world of work and behavior, a life in which the personal and the social and the private and public are not at war but at work together in God's service.

Luke tells a story (see Luke 18:18-24): A man, a devoted Jew, who inwardly, deeply wants to live a godly life, comes to see Jesus. He asks instruction: "What shall I do to inherit eternal life?" Jesus replies in the standard Jewish way, not yet choosing to point to the terrible dividedness within the man before him: "You know the commandments: 'Do not commit adultery, Do not kill, Do not steal, Do not bear false witness, Honor your father and mother.'" A smile of relief spreads across the questioner's face, for on these issues his inner life and outer life are in harmony, at one: "All these I have observed from my youth" (18:21).

When Jesus hears this, he looks with love at the deeply conflicted man before him, then speaks the words that bring the conflict to the surface: "One thing you still lack. Sell all that you have, and distribute to the poor, . . . and come, follow me"

(18:22). And with those words the alarm goes off in this rich young man's soul, for here is where the unspoken conflict lies. Here is where that phrase rises up—*I dare not:* "I DARE NOT part with the wealth and power and respect to which I've become so accustomed. Yes, I want the eternal life, the godly life to which I am inwardly drawn. At the same time, no. No, I cannot let go of the outward dressing of status, wealth, and power."

The story ends on this most unsatisfying but deeply truthful note. The conflict is not resolved. As indeed it often is not. The man is grief stricken, but not healed; no new unity is born in him. And he goes away sorrowing, inwardly wanting one life, outwardly living another.

Christ's call is always and everywhere to wholeness and to a healthy, life-giving tension in which inner wants and outward work are both joined in God's service. Have you felt the crippling division of a life lived in two opposite, unreconciled directions? Have you lived with pretense too long? Is it time to take off the disguise? Is that what God is calling you to do at this time of decision?

Notes

Chapter 1

[1] Saul Bellow, "Leaving the Yellow House," *Mosby's Memoirs and Other Stories,* (New York: Viking Press, Inc., 1968), p. 37.

[2] *Ibid.*, p. 38.

[3] *Ibid.*, p. 42.

[4] "A Losing Battle," *New York Times,* October 21, 1982, sec. B, p. 14.

[5] Carl Sandburg, "An Old Woman," *Breathing Tokens* (New York: Harcourt Brace Jovanovich, Inc., 1978) p. 56.

Chapter 2

[1] Horace Judson, *The Eighth Day of Creation* (New York: Simon & Schuster, Inc., 1979), p. 417.

[2] Woody Allen, *Side Effects* (New York: Random House, Inc., 1980) pp. 11-12.

Chapter 4

[1] Carl Sandburg, *Abraham Lincoln: The War Years,* 4 Vols. (New York: Harcourt Brace Jovanovich, Inc.), p. 385.

[2] Susan Sontag, "The Dummy," *I, Etcetera* (New York: Farrar, Straus, & Giroux, Inc., 1978), p. 93.

[3] Frederick Buechner, *The Sacred Journey* (San Francisco: Harper & Row Publishers, Inc., 1982), pp. 31-32. Reprinted by permission of Harper & Row, Publishers, Inc.

[4] Carl Sandburg, *The Complete Poems of Carl Sandburg* (New York: Harcourt Brace Jovanovich, Inc., 1970), p. 23.

[5] Aram Saroyan, *Last Rites: The Death of William Saroyan* (New York: William Morrow & Co., Inc., 1982), p. 150.

Chapter 5

[1] Anne Sexton, "Rowing," *The Awful Rowing Toward God* (Boston: Houghton Mifflin Co., 1975), pp. 1-2.

[2] Louise Bogan, *Journey Around My Room: The Autobiography of Louise Bogan,* ed. Ruth Limmer (New York: Viking Press, Inc., 1980), p. 10.

[3] *Ibid.*

[4] William Shirer, *Twentieth Century Journey* (New York: Simon & Schuster, Inc., 1976), pp. 274-275.

Chapter 6

[1] John Cheever, *Bullet Park* (New York: Alfred A. Knopf, Inc., 1969), p. 142.

[2] "Once Unflappable Auto Executives Show Stress Symptoms," *New York Times*, January 18, 1982, sec. A, p. 12.

[3] "Out for a Helluva Good Time," *Fortune*, January 21, 1981, p. 15.

Chapter 7

[1] Anne Tyler, *Dinner at the Homesick Restaurant* (New York: Alfred A. Knopf, Inc., 1982), p. 99.

[2] Saul Bellow, *Mr. Sammler's Planet* (New York: Viking Press, Inc., 1970), p. 316.

[3] Private correspondence.

Chapter 8

[1] Saul Bellow, *The Dean's December* (New York: Harper & Row Publishers, Inc., 1982), p. 266. Reprinted by permission of Harper & Row, Publishers, Inc.

[2] Herman Wouk, "You, Me, and the Novel," *Saturday Review*, June 29, 1974, p. 13.

[3] Robert Frost, "The Pauper Witch of Grafton" from "Two Witches" in *The Poetry of Robert Frost*, ed. Edward C. Lathem (New York: Holt, Rinehart & Winston, 1969).

[4] For a particularly twisted example of the "logic" used to justify the use of violence by some liberation theologians, consider the following quote from *PCR Information, Reports and Background Papers 1980/No. 4*, a publication of the World Council of Churches Programme to Combat Racism:

A good end, for example social justice, does not contain and, therefore, positively qualify the means to accomplish it. In the same way any particular means are not intrinsically just or unjust. Means also do not become unequivocally "just" when they are used for a "just" end. This is especially true for the means of violence.

In the same way, non-violence as a principle of action is not ethically "correct" in all circumstances. Whoever chooses non-violence in an escalated conflict must anticipate casualties, especially in the group working for change. Because non-violent resistance almost never achieves quick success, it requires much patience and, possibly, the continuation of an intolerable situation.

Whenever violence is understood as an instrument, the intended goal must be clearly describable and achievable within a foreseeable length of time. Only then can the appropriateness of violence as a means be measured, in the face of the possible side effects of violence. "Social justice," for example, is a human goal, which requires different kinds of partial achievements under certain conditions; hence, requires for its realization individual changes in legal, economic, or social conditions. Violence can be a rational means to an end in some circumstances only in light of such partial achievements.

[5] "Southern Baptists' Leader Assails Moderates," *New York Times*, June 15, 1982, sec. A, p. 8.

[6] "Top Baptist Bailey Smith Wins Souls and Raises Hackles," *People Weekly*, March 8, 1982, p. 87.

[7] Leonard Sweet, "Not All Cats Are Gray: Beyond Liberalism's Uncertain Faith," *Christian Century*, June 23, 1982, p. 722.

[8] Dag Hammarskjold, *Markings* (New York: Alfred A. Knopf, Inc., 1964), p. 64.

[9] C.S. Lewis, *The Screwtape Letters and Screwtape Proposes a Tape* (New York: Macmillan Publishing Co., Inc., 1982), p. 129.

Chapter 9

[1] William Least Heat Moon, *Blue Highways: A Journey into America* (Boston: Little, Brown & Company, 1983), p. 3.

Chapter 10

[1] Robert Pirsig, *Zen and the Art of Motorcycle Maintenance: An Inquiry into Values* (New York: William Morrow & Co., Inc., 1974), pp. 34-35.

[2] Thomas J. Peters and Robert H. Waterman, *In Search of Excellence: Lessons from America's Best Run Companies* (New York: Harper & Row Publishers, Inc., 1982), p. 65.

Chapter 11

[1] E.H. Erikson, *Identity: Youth and Crisis* (New York: W.W. Norton & Co., Inc., 1968), pp. 132 ff.

[2] Abigail Van Buren, *The Best of Dear Abby* (New York: Andrews & McMeel, Inc., 1981), p. 242.

[3] Wendell Berry, *A Place on Earth*, rev. (San Francisco: North Point Press, 1983), p. 150. Copyright © 1982 by Wendell Berry. Reprinted by permission.

Chapter 12

[1] Kurt Vonnegut, Jr., *Mother Night* (New York: Avon Books, 1967), p. v.

[2] J.M. Coetzee, *The Life and Times of Michael K.* (New York: Viking Press, Inc., 1983), p. 66. Copyright © 1983 by J.M. Coetzee. Reprinted by permission of Viking Penguin Inc.

[3] John Kenneth Galbraith, "Corporate Man," *New York Times Magazine*, January 22, 1984, p. 39.